AWAKENING TO

SOUL

CONSCIOUSNESS

Other Books by John W. Otis

Will the Real You Please Stand Up

Whispers from the Soul

Received from subscribers to Lessons from the Soul:

It's great to hear from you…my heart jumps up to have contact with this Light-source. I want to thank you for your inspiration and light..the oneness I am feeling is that I am happy for us all! — Janne

Thanks for telling it like it is. I hope we are all transformed by love and light soon. — Randy

I am so blessed…so privileged to receive your Light…so grateful for the energy and focus which resulted in your book. Glad to be part of the extended community. — Annata

Thank you for illuminating my path with your profound and ever unfolding heart messages. Thank you and much love. — Angelika

Your words always serve to center and calm me. They ring of truth and love. — N. C.

———————

Lessons from the Soul are messages received from the Higher Self during daily meditation. They are emailed weekly by The Eye of the Sacred Wind Foundation to subscribers around the world. This book is, in part, based on revelations from these lessons. For more information on the foundation, or to subscribe to Lessons from the Soul, please visit our web site: www.sacredwind.org.

AWAKENING TO

SOUL

CONSCIOUSNESS

*It's Time to Awaken
the Real You!*

☙

John W. Otis

Eye of the Sacred Wind Foundation
Whitefish, Montana

ISBN: 1449561950

EAN-13: 9781449561956

Cover & Book Design: Richard Kurth Design, Whitefish, Montana

Dedicated to the Inner Voice of Truth
that reveals all we need to know

Acknowledgment

It is with the deepest feeling of Love that I give thanks for the support and limitless patience of my wife and soulmate, Cheryl. Her always happy countenance has truly been a shining light in my life as we have lived, laughed and worked together as one. I am eternally thankful for her wisdom and counsel as this book on awakening of the soul was revealed and created.

John — April 30, 2009

TABLE OF CONTENTS

THE AWAKENING

You are living in an age that has been foretold for millennia, a time when there would be a transition of consciousness to an age of love and light, where mankind would awaken to the truth of existence, when peace and harmony would reign supreme throughout the world. This is that time.

As you meditate in the silence, feel the infinite flow of love and light as it moves out into and through the consciousness of the soul and through every molecule of your existence. Feel that light radiating out, connecting with other points of light within your community, in your region, in your family, in your friends, spreading across the continent, and around the world. Picture and feel the millions of points of light that are being connected at this very moment, points of light awakening, awakening.

Light has no boundary, it has no limitation. Light is infinite; it is the eternal flow of love. Wherever there is an opening to the inner awakening process, a point of light emanates. Some lights are brighter than others, but there are millions of points of light awakening, expanding in understanding. connecting with other points of light. It is happening on a grand scale. As these points of light reach a critical mass, there will be a tremendous upwelling of understanding and acceptance, and great acceleration into the golden age of light.

*So know that at this very moment you are connected with and part of that infinite global web of light. That is the true worldwide web that is now in place. This is the reality that you and millions of others around the planet are awakening to as the mask of humanhood is shed and the mantle of love and light is draped around your shoulders. This is the age of **the awakening** you have been waiting for. It's time for you to awaken to who you 'really' are.*

— Revealed from the Higher Self in meditation, March 18, 2009.

There are no end points along the pathway of Life,
only moments of revelation that propel
the soul toward the horizon of
awakened consciousness.

— Whispers from the Soul

projections of potential and possibility that will aid in opening the inner doorway of remembering who you really are. You will discover the ultimate reality of oneness and unity with all creation as you walk the pathway of awakening to soul consciousness.

Some of the terms used in this discussion may not be familiar to you. Or perhaps you may feel a partial understanding of the concepts presented. In any case, by the time you finish this book you will have a better understanding of what is meant by *consciousness, Consciousness of Creation, soul, oneness, journey of the soul, trinity of creation* and *awakening*. These are concepts that reflect the language of the soul and are fundamental to understanding the awakening process.[5]

Another concept related to understanding the awakening process is to know that you, as a soul, have passed through many lifetimes in the school of Earth. Each lifetime has provided a series of lessons. Some were learned; others had to be repeated. There is no other way. The ultimate goal of the life process through many incarnations is to fully awaken, to know and be aware of your oneness with all creation. Every moment of life is precious for within each moment lies the potential for discovering this reality. By the time you complete this book, you will remember that awakening to soul consciousness is to know and be who you really are!

We're all on a spiritual journey, seeking to know and to discover an answer to the eternal question of *who am I*. There are many clues and doorways to walk through along the way. However, the final answer to the question often remains just beyond our reach. We plod along embroiled in earthly pursuits and relationships occasionally peeking over the horizon to search

---

[5] *See Glossary for description of these and other terms used in this book as part of the language of the soul.*

for an ultimate answer. We perhaps begin to see more clearly. We expand our understanding, and then retreat into comfortable but limited belief systems and the whirlpool of human activity. We experience, we grow, we expand our awareness, we learn.

As we learn, we share what we know to be true and helpful with others who are traveling with us through this classroom called life. We're all in this adventure together. As we learn and grow in awareness, we validate the truism that *all is one*. We discover that there is only one Source, and we are all an aspect of that Source. As we awaken, we recognize the truth that all souls are on their individual journey of the soul, the only journey any of us is really on.

AWAKENING TO

SOUL

CONSCIOUSNESS

UNDERSTANDING THE MYSTERY OF CREATION

The Mystery

What if you discovered who you *really* are as a soul? What if you remembered why you are here on Earth? What if you allowed the consciousness of love to be your guiding light? What if you understood the wonder and magic of creation? Understanding the mystery of creation provides the foundation for discovering and awakening to the truth of who you *really* are.

As we observe the universe around us, we are often amazed at the complexity, beauty, and enormity of the created environment. From the micro view through powerful electronic microscopes to the macro view through radio telescopes and satellites that reach nearly to the boundary of the known universe, we see and witness an infinite array of created patterns and substance. Even the casual observer will at some point have a feeling deep within of an underlying mystery of how this created universe came into being and how it is sustained. What is it all about? It is indeed a mystery but only because the process of creation is not understood.

We see an infinite flow of creative activity throughout our three-dimensional experience. We see it in the human body, in animals and other life forms on land, in the air, and in oceans, lakes and rivers. We see amazing and seemingly infinite creativity in vegetation and plant life. Have you ever marveled at the detail and intricacies of a rose or other flower? Have you ever viewed the patterns of life activity that can only be seen through a microscope? In the fossil record of Earth, we see evidence of millions of years of evolving life forms preserved in testimony to the grand scope of creative possibility.

Much that is observed can be analyzed, described and shared in an attempt to correlate what is understood with other aspects of creation. But the mystery seems to remain for there is always the question of what is the source? What is creation really all about? And ultimately the question arises: *Who am I and why am I here?*

So there is a mystery because it seems as though the ultimate scope and purpose of creation can simply not be known. Has it ever occurred to you that somewhere there had to be an intention to form and establish the infinite landscape of creation that we witness daily? Solving the mystery of creation has been the subject of countless philosophical and religious discussions and initiatives ever since man first emerged as a thinking, feeling entity. There is ongoing debate between those who support or believe in creationism versus those who through observing the earth and its inhabitants support the concept of evolution. A visit to the internet will provide more than enough references to fuel this debate for years. This book will take a different approach looking at the mystery of creation from an inner, metaphysical perspective rather than a debate over observable results of the creation process. It is up to you, the reader, to determine if what is presented feels right at a deep and sustaining level.

Consider, if the entire created universe came from somewhere and was formed out of created substance, then there must be an underlying foundation upon which the process of creation rests. If this is true, which it appears to be, then that foundation must be the one Source of everything that exists. How can there be two sources of creation?

This one Source has been called many things – God, Allah,

the One, the Great Mystery and many other similar names. From the human perspective, it is a rather magnificent concept to realize that there is indeed a Source, a motivating energy of creation that exists everywhere. Life is considered to be a mystery when considering that the Source is infinite and beyond all possibility of being *known* and *understood* from the limited perception of the human experience. We can see evidence of the creative process, but we can't see the Source. When the term Source is used, it is not referring to a pin point or center of existence from which creation radiates outward. Rather, consider that this infinite Source is everywhere, omni-dimensional, omni-present …everywhere!

It is more of a metaphorical statement related to man's propensity for linear thinking to say that there is a beginning. For when considering an infinite statement of creation there is no beginning, there is no end. There is simply a flow of creative energy, seen and unseen, that is pervasive, everywhere, without exception. It's in the air you breathe; it's in the sunshine; it's in the light that comes from the timeless meanderings of stars and planets. It's in the water; it's in every organism, every animate and inanimate object of earthly experience. And, of course, this creative energy is in every human being; it's in everything on planet Earth, everything in the universe and beyond.

This underlying reality of an infinite creative energy that is always present is the mysterious foundation that has been the subject of countless philosophical discussions for millennia. There can be endless debate about what to call this energy. In the Eye of the Sacred Wind Foundation this energy is referred to as the *Consciousness of Creation*. It is perhaps difficult to understand how consciousness is energy. But, consider that as the energy of creation flows, it transforms consciousness, or an idea, into created form and substance. It is in the same manner that when you have an idea, an inner impulse, or an intention to create something and you take action, that impulse of energy moves from an unmanifested state into whatever is your intention to create. Consciousness, the knowing of an idea is projected, creation happens!

The flow of creative energy is a constant. You sense and feel the movement of energy in your physical body as it sustains the bodily form and function. The flow of energy passes through your mind. You feel and sense inner activity that materializes into thoughts and ideas. You feel the flow of energy when you sleep as evidenced through dreams and knowing that even when asleep your physical body is being sustained through an energy exchange.

Energy and Consciousness
It is challenging to comprehend the definition of energy, for the term energy is used in so many ways in the physical, mechanistic world. There is electrical, nuclear, and mechanical energy. Then there is reference to energy of natural resources of coal, oil, and natural gas. All of these are evidence of an internal source of energy that can be released and transformed through certain manipulations of energy producing systems. Einstein postulated that the existence of energy was the foundation for the entire universe when he developed his famous equation, $E=mc^2$ (Energy = Mass x Speed of Light^2). This equation tells us that energy and mass, or matter, are interchangeable; mass is a form of energy. This leads to the understanding that everything is a form of energy; energy is all around us and within us. It permeates everything.

The human aura, or energy field, has been observed by clairvoyants of many cultures for thousands of years. Ancient Egyptians called the subtle body the *ka*, a luminous entity which would separate from the physical body at the point of death.

Plato called this life energy *nous* and Aristotle called it *entelecheia*. Early Christian saints were painted with the aura, or halo, surrounding the head. In recent years there has been increasing research into subtle energies that are part of the bioelectric field of energy that permeates and surrounds living bodies and other organisms.[6] These subtle energies have been known by mystics and healers around the world for many centuries. In China this energy is *qi*; in India it's *prana*; in Hawaii it's *mana*; the Native Americans call it *Great Spirit*.

There are also various protocols of energy healing projected through the mind, intentional prayer, or through the hands in such healing practices as Reiki and therapeutic massage. There are those known as medical intuitives who are attuned to the infinite web of energy and consciousness and offer an extended perspective of energetic healing.[7] In these practices, there is a transfer of energy that brings about a greater alignment of harmony and balance in the physical body.

With increased understanding of quantum physics,[8] the concept of energy as it relates to consciousness has been greatly expanded. A simplified description of the relationship between energy and quantum physics reveals that since everything is made of energy, all apparent and observable realities are created by thoughts that hold the energy in place. There are infinite possibilities that exist and it is the observer that creates the reality that is seen and

---

[6] *To read more on the history of the aura and the merging of science and metaphysics, go to Pioneers of the Aura at KarenMutton.com.*

[7] *A Medical Intuitive uses a variety of methods to determine the health or emotional problem of a client including clairvoyance (clear vision), clairaudience (clear hearing), clairsentience (clear sensing), and prophetic knowing. There are many resources on the internet about medical intuitives and training programs.*

[8] *Quantum physics is the branch of physics based on quantum theory which is the theoretical basis of modern physics that explains the nature and behavior of matter and energy on the atomic and subatomic level.*

experienced. Our reality is dependent on our belief systems that filter what we manifest thus limiting the possibilities we see and experience.[9]

Ultimately the flow of energy is a rather profound concept when related to what is often referred to as universal intelligence, or infinite consciousness, the sustaining life force that gives structure and meaning to creation. There is also the flow of energy that is not physical such as thought forms that are projected, received and felt. Have you ever thought about someone only to have the phone ring and there they are? Or, have you made contact with someone and heard them say, *I was just thinking about you.* There are multiple examples throughout history where the same concept or idea simultaneously came to the surface of awareness in two or more people that had no physical connection with each other.[10] The energy of creation, or consciousness, is always present in both manifested and unmanifested forms and ideas.

Energy is not easily defined as evidenced by the multiple ways in which energy is observed, described and measured. Energy is a profound universal statement of the flow of consciousness present as the sustaining energy of all creation. Again, in this book this infinite sustaining energy is referred to as the *Consciousness of Creation*.

Different words and concepts applied to what is viewed as the one Source reflect the needs and understanding at the moment of those who are searching and wondering. They know there is something beyond the limitations of physical and mental creations. They know there is a Source, a foundation supporting all creation. As words are used, the assumed meaning being shared is diluted

---

[9] *For more information on energy and consciousness see The Energy Healing Experiments, Gary Swartz PhD, Simon and Schuster, 2008.*

[10] *See The New Yorker, May 12, 2008: In the Air-Who Says Big Ideas Are Rare? by Malcolm Gladwell.*

by the biases, belief systems, or limited perception of whoever is hearing or reading the words. It must be understood that words are symbolic and indicative, not absolute, as there is always a meaning behind the meaning being suggested by every word.

When the word *consciousness* is used, it is important to recognize that the underlying reality of consciousness is infinite. It has no boundaries. It has no limitations. It is a qualitative statement of simply being and knowing. This is not easily interpreted by the mind as we often limit understanding due to perceptions we hold formed by experience. There are different words used in an attempt to define consciousness, but words cannot define what is infinite and indefinable. Words do not change the reality of an infinite Source of creative energy, or the Consciousness of Creation.

Words point the way, they are not the destination. What is important is to understand that there is indeed a foundation to our existence. There is a flow of energy, a flow of creative and sustaining consciousness. This energy, or consciousness, is applied in multiple ways with the result being what we observe in the physical and material world. The Consciousness of Creation is everywhere. Is that not a comforting thought? For wherever you are, you are in the midst of the flow of creative energy. The Consciousness of Creation is always present.

There is a tendency within the human experience to think and act in a linear, hierarchical manner. This tendency can be seen in organized religion, social, cultural, and political structures. It manifests in the need of the embodied soul to feel attached to and in control of its environment, its history, its background, and its future. The flow of consciousness is not linear. Consciousness has no form; it has no boundaries or limitations. It is simply everywhere. We need to move away from linear or hierarchical thinking for that is not the way the universe works.

Linear thinking retains fixed points of focus within a three dimensional framework of reference. In order to move beyond those points of reference, it is necessary to be open to an expanded concept. Consider a spiral. It is a particular form of energy flow that starts from a given point, moves out, never ending, always expanding. If one needed a symbol, the spiral would be a good one to ponder as it provides an excellent visualization of the movement of infinite energy, or consciousness. Is it surprising that various forms of the spiral are found in archeological sites of early cultures throughout the world? There has always been a need to search for a reference point somewhere beyond the immediate physical world. The spiral symbolizes the age-old quest to find this reference point.

Consider the Consciousness of Creation as spiraling energy moving in the infinite pattern of creation. All energy spirals as can be seen in solar systems, galaxies and star patterns throughout the universe. It can be seen within the chakras and energy patterns of the human body. It can be seen within the energy of the atom. There are no straight lines in the universe, only spiraling, moving energy, or consciousness.

The one constant in your existence is the flow of consciousness, for consciousness is always moving in and through that which is created. Consciousness is knowing; consciousness is awareness; consciousness is being; consciousness is the essence of the reality of creation. Consciousness is like the wind that moves through the trees. You feel the wind, you often hear it, you sense it, you experience it, but you don't see it. It is the cause of that which you observe, see, feel and sense. The process of creation is similar, it never ceases, has no beginning, has no end, is omni-dimensional, and omni-present. You see the results of creation but only feel the cause.

Once again referring to quantum physics, it can be seen that everything is made of energy. We are creating every moment of our existence consistent with our perceptions within the unlimited possibilities of infinite universal intelligence. Our creation is only limited by our belief systems and tenacity to hold on to what has been created. We discover that we can change our creation as we awaken to the expanded understanding of who we really are.

Creation is a continuum that has always been and will always be. You are a part of the continuum of creation as you move along the journey of the soul. We are in an age when the time has arrived for the soul to awaken to its true character and nature! It is time to solve the mystery of creation.

2

IT'S TIME TO SOLVE THE MYSTERY

What is stopping people throughout the world from feeling oneness and connectedness to each other and to the planet? Why do so many hesitate to go deeply within to discover who they really are? What is stopping people from awakening and discovering the answer to *who am I*? Many people are, in fact, answering the call and walking the path of awakening, but why are there so many who don't respond or don't even know a call has gone out? There is no one answer to these questions. Rather there seem to be a number of contributing factors that cloud inner vision and create points of resistance to the awakening process.

One major factor is a tendency to hold onto ideas, belief systems, concepts and physical attachments that seem so real and important. These aspects of creation seem so tangible and we vigorously defend our possession of them. We build up a crust of resistance to change. A veil of illusion is created that gives the worldly activities a sense of permanence as an assumed reality. As the flow of truth emerges from the depths of soul consciousness, the points of resistance begin to dissolve. A transformation takes place. There is a break through the resistance that has been built up over many lifetimes of experience. It is like awakening into a new day, into a new awareness of who and why you are as a soul.

It is important to be honest with yourself as you consider what it is that still pulls your attention into the nooks and crannies of human experience. What is it in your physical, emotional, mental life that you are still attracted to? What is it that you are still attached to? What is it that you resist letting go of? Is it an emotional or physical need or attraction? Is it a mental or intellectual craving? What is it that holds your attention?

Attachment

Attachment to things of the world is a sometimes nebulous, sometimes direct, other times subtle form of holding on to an assumed reality. It is easy to become attached to *things* for we live in a physical world and have certain needs. We fulfill our needs with a wide variety of products and objects that become very much a part of our existence. Of course, there is nothing wrong with using and having physical objects since existing in the world in which we live requires us to have certain things that are an important part of day to day activities.

The subtle trap lies in becoming attached to those things where they become more important than the process of life you are passing through. Often the attachment is emotional. It just feels good to have or to be around a particular physical object. These are often personal possessions, perhaps items that have been passed down from previous generations. Or they are things that suggest a level of accomplishment, an award recognized by others, or something you have created. There are many ways that emotions can ensnare and trap you into becoming attached to the objects of life. Again, a subtle but potential trap that needs to be recognized.

It is also easy to become attached to other people, to form an emotional attachment that creates a dependency where one abdicates personal responsibility for self discovery by transferring their identity onto someone else. This attachment becomes a very tentative and paper-thin reality.

There is also attachment to fear about the life process and an unknown future. Fear is a response to a lack of understanding, a lack of knowing who you are, knowing that you, as a soul, are a spark of the Consciousness of Creation. When you go within and touch the link in consciousness between who you really are and what the rest of the world is, fear disappears. For what is there to be afraid of in the infinite realm of spirit? Fear is a dramatic outgrowth of attachment and has to be recognized as transitory and temporary.

Fear can be eliminated with a willingness to move inward in recognition of the truth of one's being. This takes a great deal of dedication and work, but the trip is worth the price. It is the only trip worth taking. For one who is imbedded in an aura of fear, it is necessary to release those attachments and perceptions that generate fear. Life is what it is, a magnificent journey of learning, experiencing, growing, coming into the fullness of awakening to the truth of who you are as a soul. What is there to fear? Nothing! Fear is a pattern of habit, another subtle hurdle to get across when one becomes attached to things, feelings and emotions. The only solution is to discover who you really are. Then, in an instant, fear disappears never again to be a concern in the life process.

Sometimes there are attachments to other people's dreams and possibilities which can be the proverbial house built on sand. Trying to live someone else's dream is being attached to an illusion. It is like trying to put your arms around a wispy cloud that passes through the atmosphere of experience. As the atmosphere changes, the cloud changes, the form changes, and sometimes it even disappears. It is always important to live the life that you have chosen in order to experience that which you need to experience to awaken into the fullness of knowing who you are. Know that you are doing the right things for the right reasons.

So consider how important it is to become unattached to the things of life and to recognize that the truth of who you are lies within. Attachments need to be seen for what they are: shadows of true reality. You see, this is part of the process of identifying what it is that has attracted you to this lifetime, what it is that you are challenged to release, to let go of. Consider your activities, your feelings, your perceptions, your emotional responses, and you will be able to understand where the tentacles of attachment still exist. As previously stated, the pathway is to be in the world but not of it. We are not suggesting to summarily leave the world or to not participate in worldly affairs. After all, that's why you're here, to be part of and to enthusiastically experience your created environment. The point is to strive to understand the world more clearly, to allow the world to be what it is but not to be attached or over reactive to it.

As you walk the pathway of awakening, you need to allow resistance to the world to dissolve. We often have belief systems based on the temporal nature of our existence that hold us in bondage. These belief systems often have fixed notions and rules with rigid boundaries. Part of awakening is allowing your beliefs to be flexible as there is an evolution of increased awareness. You will recognize the outer assumed reality for what it is and will allow a clearer understanding of reality to emerge by releasing points of resistance. The awakening process is an inner revolution, an inner evolution, and an inner revelation opening the inner doorway of remembering who you are as a soul.

It is important to not allow outer conditions to dominate your perceptions and growing understanding of who you are. The inner flow of expanding awareness needs to become the dominant focus in thoughts generated, words spoken, and action taken. This enables you to move through your present environment aware of who you are and what you are doing from an inner perspective of awakened truth.

There is another factor that relates to understanding the relationship between inner and outer realities. To the degree there is attachment to what is created, you activate within your applied consciousness what is often called ego. Ego is an attachment to the world of limited perception and is not a permanent component of the consciousness of the soul. Ego presents a clouded vision of reality that wants to hold on to what is created perhaps because of fear of losing an assumed identity, doubt about what's truly real, lack of understanding, or because of a desire to be in control and be recognized for what the ego thinks it is creating in the outer world.

This is all part of the created environment. To the extent that one looks into the mirror of existence and says *I am apart from, I am separate from all that is around me,* the ego becomes fully active. It says *I am important, I am reality, and I am in charge.* But the ego is not permanent. It represents a temporary attachment to limited perception and limited consciousness. The ego lives in the world of duality; the soul exists in the reality of oneness.[11]

The degree of attachment and reaction to what is created is a clear indication of whether or not you live within boundaries of limited perception. How attached are you to the created environment? Is unity and oneness with the world around you felt and understood, or is there a sense of separateness and multiplicity? As you walk the pathway of awakening, the ego will diminish in importance as you release attachments to the assumed importance of the world and its ways. The ego will eventually disappear as limited perceptions are dissolved and you remember who you really are.

This is called the vanquishing of the ego, an important step along the pathway of awakening. As the ego disappears, there is no longer a perceived separation between inner and outer reality. You recognize there is a thread of connectedness running through

---

[11] *The concept of 'oneness' is discussed in detail in Chapter 8.*

everything you see and experience. All is seen as creative energy being expressed in a multitude of ways. Everything is seen as emanating from and a part of the Source, the Consciousness of Creation.

The Trinity of Human Endeavor
To assist in resolving the challenge to move beyond limitations of an ego-based approach to life, it is helpful to consider the *Trinity of Human Endeavor*. If your observations and expectations about the life process are somewhat fixed and inflexible, this trinity will undoubtedly be faced over and over again until mastered.

The first part of this trinity is *expectations*. Expectations generate an illusory, limited perception of the life process. Potential becomes crystallized and restricted as expectations place boundaries around one's thoughts, emotions, and mental projections. We often have expectations of how others should act, what they should or should not say, what they should believe. We also often have rigid notions about how certain conditions of life should or should not be. Having fixed expectations limits the potential for creative spontaneity and for the wonder of synchronicity in events and relationships.

The second part of this trinity is *reaction*. What is a reaction? It is a response to an unfulfilled expectation! When we have expectations that are not fulfilled in the way *we* want, there is often a reaction such as *I wanted the outcome of the event to be different*, or *they should have acted or spoken differently*, or a variety of other responses. Reactions reinforce a limited perception of the flow of life energy. Reactions generally involve our emotions which when activated pull our attention and focus into the web of human endeavor. This emotional response is enervating and tends to hold awareness in bondage to outer conditional activities.

Eventually the soul wants to move from responses to life that are conditional upon outer stimulus to an unconditional response to the flow of love energy from within. This shift in focus is amplified when one is consciously on the pathway of awakening.

The third part of the *Trinity of Human Endeavor*, that of *attachment*, has already been discussed. In our human experience, we find it easy to become attached to the *things* of life. We become possessive of physical objects. We wrap our minds and emotions around certain dogmas and traditions. We even subtly become attached to other people and what we think they represent in our life. Attachments are the glue of life that to a measure keep us focused on outer relationships and structures. This prevents the roots of awakening from penetrating very deeply into evolving soul awareness.

To resolve these aspects of human endeavor, we need to transform these three legs of the *Trinity of Human Endeavor* into unlimited potential and possibility. We first need to transform *expectations* into *anticipation*. We need to recognize that the highest and best good for all is potentially available within every relationship, every activity, and every occurrence. This requires a transformation of thinking from one of limitation to one of unlimited possibilities, anticipating the most productive and positive outcome of every event. It means waking up in the morning and saying *what a beautiful day this is with potential for wondrous things to occur*. We need to transform *expectations* with related boundaries and limitations into *anticipation* that opens the doorway of potential for the flow of infinite creative energy as part of all we are involved in. We anticipate the excitement of synchronicity and unexpected events and chance meetings to occur. Life is lived enthusiastically with unlimited potential to realize intentions for this lifetime.

We then need to transform *reaction* into *response*. We learn to respond to events and conditions of life from an inner understanding rather than what might be called a *knee-jerk* reaction based on emotions and expectations. We respond to situations or events by perhaps saying *how interesting* or *I wonder what the meaning is behind what happened*, rather than offering an emotional, ego-centered response because expectations were not fulfilled. Responding in this way stimulates increased understanding and the potential for insights into the current experience. We need to transform emotionally-based *reactions* into unattached and unconditional *responses* that allow for the infinite potential of love and light to flow unimpeded as the awakening process continues.

The third step is to transform *attachment* to *appreciation*. We learn to appreciate all aspects of the flow of creative energy without being attached to the form or substance of the process. We discover that there is deep-seated value in being detached from ego-driven needs, physical objects, fixed notions and ideas, and attachment to others. Being detached from the world means different things to different people. To some, it implies becoming a recluse, denying the *things* of life, perhaps living in a remote area, maybe even a monastery. To others, it means following a particular focus of spiritual or religious persuasion supported with dogma and traditions that enforce a detachment from worldly matters. And to others it means to simply be in the world but not attached to it.

We need to recognize that all aspects of creation have merit and inherent value. We learn that we really don't own anything. We came into this life experience without much, and we'll eventually leave this life without much other than the experiences and lessons learned. However, we can appreciate whatever we have had the privilege of having access to and being exposed to during our lifetime. We need to transform *attachment* into *appreciation* which allows us to experience the potential for understanding and participating in the infinite variety of life's creative adventure.

Mastering the *Trinity of Human Endeavor* opens ever wider the inner doorway of awakening to soul consciousness. Within every moment of life lies the potential for resolving the challenges of humanhood as you walk the pathway of transforming *expectation into anticipation, reaction into response*, and *attachment into appreciation*. When you are committed to mastering this trinity, you find that you enter each day with the anticipation of walking in the radiance of love and light, in peace and harmony with yourself, your family, your friends and all who cross your path. You anticipate actions to occur that lead toward fulfillment of your intentions for this lifetime. You respond with sensitivity and compassion to all events of the day. You appreciate the wonder and marvel of the created environment you are part of. Life becomes an exciting and fulfilling adventure.

The Trinity of Creation – Love, Light, Life

There are many other trinities that we see in our life experience. It is not by accident that we exist in a *three-dimensional* environment. We are here to fully experience the challenge of living in a world of duality while being exposed to the expanded reality of oneness One of the most important trinities to know and integrate into our awareness is the *Trinity of Creation: Love, Light and Life*

The *Trinity of Creation* points the way toward a deeper understanding of the journey of the soul. Since we are in a three-dimensional universe it makes sense that our understanding of who and why we are should be in the context of where we are at the moment. Hence the concept of a trinity makes sense.

Love is a powerful word used on many levels of understanding. From the universal perspective, love just is, light just is, and life just is. It has been said that *God is Love*, or stated another way, the

Consciousness of Creation is Love. How true, but how misunderstood. Love is so much more than what is generally perceived from a human perspective. Love is the foundation upon which all creation rests. Love *is* the common denominator of all soul experience. Love is the Source, love is the process, love is! How simple, but how easily missed when viewed from the limited perspective of human love which is often based on emotions with an expectation of something in return when love or affection is shared. Infinite universal love is unselfish and unconditional.

When we consider light in the three-dimensional world, we see what is called the visible spectrum that is defined as electromagnetic radiation with a wavelength of about 4,000 to 7,700 angstroms[12] that can be perceived by the normal unaided human eye. Beyond the visible spectrum, light is referred to as electromagnetic radiation of any wavelength. In the field of quantum physics, light is seen as both a wave and a particle referred to as the photon, a subatomic particle, the quanta of electromagnetic radiation. Many scientists in the field of quantum physics are involved in ongoing research and experimentation to determine a clearer definition of light.

From a metaphysical perspective, *light* is more than just the colors of the visible spectrum. Light is seen as an infinite wave of energy that carries love into every dimension of creation. This pure infinite light of creation has been referred to as *white light.* It is perhaps more correct to say that the light of creation is pure and colorless; it is the energy that carries the Consciousness of Creation into manifestation. Without light, there is darkness; where there is light, there is no darkness. This is true on both the physical and the inner spiritual level. Remember, words are

---

[12] *An angstrom is an internationally recognized unit of length equal to 0.1 nanometer or 1 x 10 $^{-10}$ meters used in natural sciences for expressing the sizes of atoms and wavelengths of electromagnetic radiation.*

not absolute and definitive. Words point the way but the true meaning behind the words needs to be intuitively felt from an inner perspective.

As love and light energy flow into creation, the result is *life*. It can be said that love is the Source, light is the carrier wave or energy of creation, and life is the result. It is only through the soul that the love and light of creation can be discovered, experienced, and known. The soul is a spark of the divine essence of the love and light of the Consciousness of Creation. The ultimate destiny path of a soul is to discover this truth and to live it fully.

There are many divergent paths that take the focus of the soul into emotional, mental and physical activities of life. Experiences on these paths have only one purpose, and that is to bring the soul's attention back to the inner consciousness of pure love and light. This is a time for all embodied souls, cultures, races, religions and nations to come together in a unified understanding of a common foundation for existence.

The spark of love is within everyone, sometimes lying dormant and unrecognized, but always waiting for the awakening to occur. The radiance of light is in everyone, always present as the carrier wave of energy into every cell of creation. The reality of life is present in everyone, moving in and through the mind, emotions and physical vehicle of the body. All is one. There is no longer *you and me*, only *us*. We need to encourage each other to remember this profound truth. We are all, in our own way, on the pathway of remembering that love, light and life are the *Trinity of Creation.*

Understanding the *Trinity of Human Endeavor* and the *Trinity of Creation* helps solve the mystery of creation. We find an underlying purpose and foundation to life that translates to the identity and purpose for the soul. We're here as embodied souls experiencing life, remembering that we each are on the journey of the soul. It is time to awaken to this truth.

3
THE SOUL, PART ONE

The term *soul* has been used in various ways over time to refer to an elusive, hidden, ethereal, metaphysical inner connection reflecting a spiritual identity. There are many interpretations of soul with many books written on soul recovery, the journey of the soul and similar themes. All of these reflect part of the answer to what a soul really is. Finding that answer has been the goal and search of countless religions and spiritual teachings that have assisted millions of people over the centuries to find a comfortable, though not always totally satisfying, answer to what is a soul.

Plato, for instance, drawing on the words of his teacher Socrates, considered the soul as the essence of a person that decides how we behave. He considered this essence, or soul, as an incorporeal, eternal occupant of our physical being. As bodies die the soul is continually reborn in subsequent bodies. Aristotle, following Plato, defined the soul as the core essence of a being but had a differing concept of the immortality of the soul. The Persian Muslim philosopher, Avicenna, stated *"…that the soul should not be seen in relative terms, but as a primary given, a substance."* And then Thomas Aquinas in the 13th century produced the *Summa Theologica* in which he offered a full argument for the immortality of the soul.

The *Bahá'í Faith* affirms that *the soul is a sign of God, a heavenly gem whose reality the most learned of men hath failed to grasp, and whose mystery no mind, however acute, can ever hope to unravel.*

Bahá'u'lláh stated that the soul not only continues to live after the physical death of the human body, but is, in fact, immortal.

In the Christian faith, there are several interpretations of what soul may or may not be depending on which dogma one accepts. Every religious faith has dealt with the concept of soul including Hinduism, Islam, Jainism, Judaism and others. There is no unified or agreed upon concept of soul. From this it can be seen that even though there has been no singular definition of soul, every religious and spiritual discipline has tried to explain what it is that is just beyond the boundary of the physical, mental and emotional existence of man.

The Soul Unveiled

What follows is a discussion of *soul* that is intended to fill in some of the gaps in understanding and assist in answering the question of *who and why am I?*

When the word *soul* is used, consider that this refers to you as a conscious entity embodied in this lifetime to experience creation and remember who you *really* are. Here's a revelation of truth that may at first be difficult to understand and accept. But, once understood and realized, much about the mystery of creation and your place in the scheme of things begins to make sense:

> *You are a soul within a body, not a body with a soul!*
> *The soul is the Consciousness of Creation in motion!*

Have you ever wondered how you and other souls have come into human bodies on Earth over many lifetimes? It is a very interesting process that is intuitively understood as you begin to awaken and remember that you are a soul with a body, a spark of the Consciousness of Creation in motion, not a human with a soul.

You have entered into the earth experience to create, to manifest and learn as you refine your awareness and align with the inner truth of who you *really* are.[13] Earth has an accommodating environment where souls can experience what they have helped create. It is an environment well- suited to the development of soul awareness. Souls can incarnate in human form to gain experience in the wonderful classroom of Earth as they walk the pathway of remembering and awakening.

The bodily form best suited to soul experience on Earth evolved over time. The human body, or *Earth suit*, evolved in a variety of sizes, shapes, colors and bodily conditions each providing the necessary environment for a specific soul experience. The body is a temporary vehicle with the mental, emotional and physical tools to fully engage in the creative process. It is important to always remember that you are first and foremost a soul, not the body.

Over many lifetimes, souls forgot the interrelationship between various aspects of created life. Both the external physical environment and the internal state of soul awareness were affected due to a pollution of thought and action. We are now in an age when we are reassessing our relationship with all aspects of creation – with each other, with the emerging awareness of our true spiritual nature, and with the environment and natural resources of Earth.

Souls continue to come to Earth to learn, to remember and awaken to a greater awareness of who and why they are. It is estimated that the population of Earth will be over seven billion sometime in 2012. This expansion of soul population is directly related to the acceleration of awakening as the new golden age of living in harmony and peace as conscious beings of love and

---

[13] *See a Lesson from the Soul received in meditation entitled 'What is a Soul - What is Creation' in Appendix D.*

light is to be realized. More and more souls want to witness and be involved in this transition of consciousness. It is important to know that this is a time of cleansing, a time of refining, a time of integration of soul consciousness into one's awareness.

We who are experiencing Earth at this time have a soul-directed assignment and responsibility to create an aura of cleansing, an aura of peacefulness and harmony, a consciousness of love and light throughout the planet. As this occurs, there will be a realignment of our relationship to both the outer environment of Earth and the inner awareness of who we are as a soul. There will be harmonious interaction with all creation as nothing stands alone. All is connected, all is one. The awakened soul is conscious of this connectedness and knows how the creative process was originally intended to be expressed and lived, in harmony and balance. This is our birthright, our self-directed assignment, our responsibility. It is our destiny. Consider what you see around you and then project the thoughts, feelings and understanding that can modify and correct the imbalances so prevalent on Earth. Observe the resultant impact on your personal environment and consciousness of existence.

You have experienced many aspects of existence over many lifetimes. There is much that has been resolved, much that has been recognized as being of the world and released, and much that has pushed open the inner doorway of awareness a little wider. There are also emotions and things of the world that have been held on to. As long as you are still in this life cycle, there is always more to be experienced, understood, released and integrated into your awareness. There is always more to remember. It is time to awaken to the truth of who you really are, a soul, embodied on Earth for the current lifetime, one with the consciousness of Earth and all creation. The time to awaken is now; that is why you are here.

Conscious Immortality

There seems to be a strong, nearly magnetic attraction to what is created. It is as though the created environment is the entire reality of existence. In a way that is true. One's limited perception of existence determines the reality of the moment. As the soul moves through the life process, points of reality within the world of matter modify and change. New parameters of perception and new expressions come into focus. To the extent that one is aware of the changing apparent reality of one's existence, the question arises: if all is changing, what is permanent? Is there a foundation that connects all externalized expressions? The answer is revealed as the soul begins to consciously walk the inner pathway of awakening to soul consciousness. Here's an exercise that helps to explain the movement of soul energy.

Visualize a sphere of infinite magnitude with an infinite radiation of energy extending outward from the center of that sphere. The center represents the Consciousness of Creation. Consider that each of the rays of emanation is a soul moving on a ray of conscious energy building, creating, developing, and establishing a created, materialized environment. There is interaction between the various rays, or souls, as well as with what has been created. The created experience reflects the perceptions and understanding of the soul. So as perception expands, the outer created environment changes. The soul recognizes that it is a soul with a created body, not a body with a soul. The soul knows that somewhere deep within the roots of consciousness is a common link that connects all rays of energy throughout the infinite sphere of creation. The soul then begins a journey of remembering who it is.

As *the awakening* takes place, one begins to question *who am I*, and consciously begins the journey back to an awareness of the root of consciousness. The soul sees that the physical, emotional, and mental world is not permanent. When the soul understands that the only permanency of existence is within the depths of soul consciousness, the doorway opens to understanding immortality. The soul remembers that it is one with and part of the infinite flow of the Consciousness of Creation from which all creative energy emanates.

The soul is indeed immortal for how can that which is an aspect of the infinite source of creation be other than immortal? Creation is and will always be; the soul knows that it is one with the source and will always be. As this foundational truth of existence is known, the soul emerges from the web of attachment to the world and walks in conscious immortality. The soul knows who it is. The created environment is seen for what it is, a collection of props in the classroom of life. As lessons are learned, new props appear. Eventually the externalized props are no longer needed as the soul graduates to the realization of being an immortal aspect of the Consciousness of Creation. Conscious immortality is a statement of truth that all souls merge with as they awaken.

As awareness expands, it becomes obvious that there is something of a sustaining nature within each of us; that is what is called the soul, an aspect of and part of the infinite continuum of the creative process. The flow of consciousness, or creative energy, is never interrupted. There is never a time when the Consciousness of Creation does not exist. This suggests that there is never a time when the soul does not exist. Knowing this to be so brings one closer to understanding immortality.

When the notion of immortality is approached from the worldly perspective of physical, emotional, and mental references, it is a difficult concept to understand. However, when approached from the perspective of the soul, immortality is seen as an expression of oneness with the infinite continuum of the flow of creative consciousness. You discover that you, as a soul, are an immortal, eternal part of the infinite creative impulse.

The Curious Soul

As you begin to awaken, there seems to be an innate curiosity about the meaning of life and your place in the scheme of things. You reflect on how you interact with what you feel about the world around you and know that you are much more than an object within three-dimensional human experience. The fact that you can consider such a potential brings you closer to realizing that it is only through the consciousness of the soul that there can begin to be a glimmer of understanding about the infinite pattern of creative energy, always moving, always flowing, no beginning, no end.

Once this notion is grasped, you begin to see that it is only through the consciousness of the soul that questions about one's existence can be asked. No other created form in our three-dimensional world can pose questions about who and why they are. This then reveals the purpose of the soul - to explore, to interact with, to be part of and then understand the infinite flow of creativity.

What a wondrous understanding to come to. You are an embodied soul experiencing creation in order to awaken and remember who you are. This understanding offers you an opportunity to interact with each and every moment of existence from a perspective that stretches far beyond three-dimensional existence. You realize that you are a pinpoint of consciousness that feels and knows your connection with the infinite process of creation.

The Soul's Purpose

Every soul enters into a life experience with a purpose known from the very beginning. It is part of a grand design for the soul to consciously align and unite in oneness with other souls, with all of creation, and with the Consciousness of Creation.

The purpose for which a soul comes into a lifetime may be very broad with many possible avenues of exploration, or it may be very specific. Every soul, when in a quiet reflective moment, has the potential to open the inner doorway to discover why it is here. The *busy-ness* of life with a multitude of daily challenges pulls the soul's attention to the outer realm of experience often causing the soul to forget its purpose. It must be remembered, however, that the soul is always moving along the pathway of remembering its oneness and consciously reuniting with the one Source of all. Sometimes the progress is rapid, sometimes not. But the point is that every soul enters the earth experience for a reason; there is purpose to existence. The ultimate purpose will be achieved at some point in awakening to soul consciousness whether in the current lifetime or the next.

The purpose for a given lifetime is based on previous experiences carried forward by the soul from past incarnations. The soul is the sum total of all previous experiences. That is how learning takes place. The soul carries forward that which was incomplete or not fully learned in a previous lifetime; the lessons must be repeated. That's the way it works. You can never escape the result of your actions and your link with the material world.

You will always be tempted and challenged to modify your perceptions and become attached to the result of what you create in the physical, manifested world. It is important to know that the physical world is just a sign post pointing the way, providing avenues of exploration so that you, as a soul, will understand the true character and nature of your being. From the human perspective, the truth of who you are is often hidden behind a veil of misunderstanding of why you have entered into the physical realm.

The individual life purpose of each soul is very specific. When one awakens to and understands that purpose, there are inner fireworks of recognition of being aligned with and aware of the purpose for this particular life experience. Conversely, when one is involved in activities and a pattern of living that are contrary to the soul's purpose, there is often discomfort, agitation, and other external responses challenging the soul to get back on track. You need to understand your reactions to the life process by going within to discover why you are facing certain situations.

It is important to be sensitive to and aware of the pattern of life being lived. Within every event there is a hidden meaning pointing toward one's purpose for being here. There is a pattern always unfolding allowing the soul to freely and consciously realign with the purpose for the current life experience. The link between the soul's inner purpose and what is being externally lived is revealed. As you open the inner doorway of understanding there is alignment with the purpose of why you have come into this life experience. You will walk an invigorating, stimulating, energy filled, love filled, peaceful, and purposeful path as you proceed toward ultimate realignment with the oneness of all creation.

So there you are. You are more than who you think you are. You are more than what you feel you are. You are more than what you physically see yourself to be. You are an immortal soul, a beautiful statement of the presence of love and light embodied on Earth, a facet on the infinite diamond of the Consciousness of Creation. The soul cannot be completely defined in words, nor can a picture be painted that depicts what the soul truly is, for it is beyond three-dimensional representation. It is a rather broad and inclusive statement to say that as a soul you are an immortal and infinite being, but that is who you are!

It has been said in many ways in spiritual teachings that a

goal of the journey of the soul is *to be in the world but not of it.* We are in three-dimensional existence for a reason, to participate in and learn from the creative process. At the same time we are admonished not to be attached to what we create. We also need to consider that as a soul we are *in the body but not of it.* The physical body is the vehicle of the creative process used to manifest physical creation through application of thoughts, ideas and feelings. The soul is the flow of consciousness that animates and utilizes the body for the purpose of engaging in the creative process. You are not the body. You are the consciousness of the soul utilizing and moving through bodily functions.

Consider what is happening when you think, feel, project a thought, or comment on something you observe. Who or what is doing that? Is it the body, or some inner motivating energy that is moving in and through the body? When the body dies to the world, the body no longer has the ability to do these things. There is something within the body utilizing the mind, emotions and the physical vehicle responding to life's patterns. Who or what is that something? This *something* is the soul temporarily residing in the body experiencing the many aspects of the creative process. That *something* is you, the *real you.*

Edgar Cayce, known as the Sleeping Prophet in the early 20th century, said it well stating that *spirit is the cause, the mind is the builder, and the physical is the result.* In other words, the soul motivates thought and action through the mind, consistent with an underlying soul intention that manifests in the physical world. It is the goal of the soul to recognize and remember who it is and that its fundamental intention is to be a living example in the world of love and light with every thought, word and action.

The Awakening Soul
These may be difficult concepts to grasp. It may take an initial

leap of faith and understanding to move beyond the boundaries of three-dimensional thinking to the infinite, unlimited space of pure consciousness in action. But the time has come to awaken and take that leap. You want answers to the question of ultimate reality and the meaning of life. You want to experience, to learn, to know and remember who you really are. This yearning to know is embedded in the soul's purpose for this lifetime. The awakening soul wants to know!

Currently we are experiencing a wave of expanding consciousness on Earth as people around the world have heard the call and are responding. It is called *the awakening.* You are part of that awakening as you remember that you are a soul, a spark of the infinite continuum of creation walking down the pathway of awakening to soul consciousness. The journey of the soul is a wondrous and fantastic journey. *It's the only journey you are really on!*

Every soul is on an eternal quest to find the inner link that connects the infinite energy of love and light with the outer consciousness of living in the world. This link is embedded deeply within the consciousness of the soul under many layers of assumed reality that need to be penetrated, dissolved and released. The quest to find the answer to *who am I* is the ultimate purpose for the soul's existence.

There are many outer cloaks of consciousness and awareness, outer attachments to the physical, emotional, and mental world that need to be discarded and eliminated. As the soul passes through various portals of understanding, the inner truth is known and the outer cloaks of assumed reality disappear. They no longer have a leg to stand on for all is seen exactly for what it is. It is through experiencing outer conditions that inner revelations become more abundantly clear and the outer assumed reality of the life process becomes more clearly known for what it is.

In the grand symphony of awakening taking place there are many points of focus. When all outer expressions blend together into the harmonious symphony of creation there is one ultimate tone often referred to as OM.[14] The perceived sound of OM is often used in meditation. OM is the fundamental energy pattern of universal sound. Contained within the sound vibration of OM are all the aspects and resonance of the energy of creation. The pathway of awakening becomes broader and more clearly perceived as the sound of OM penetrates and is absorbed by the consciousness of the awakening soul. The soul hears and feels the sound and vibration of the infinite energy of creation, the energy of love and light. As the eternal quest continues, the awakening soul consciously connects with the inner link of understanding and knows the truth of existence.

The soul knows that each moment is very precious; it is time to fully awaken to soul consciousness. Life is a beautiful experience to be lived in peace and harmony radiating love and light, with purpose and understanding. When you are consistently on the pathway of fulfilling your purpose chosen for this lifetime, life is lived effortlessly. Everything you need is always available. Those whom you need to be with instantly appear at the moment of need. Life is full and complete.

---

[14] *In the Yoga tradition, Om (or Aum) is the supreme mantra, the most sacred of holy words. Although it is first found in the spiritual writings of Hinduism, Om is used by Buddhists and Jains in their rituals and meditation, and has also passed over into the Jewish, Christian, and Moslem religions in the form of Amin (Amen), which is intoned at the end of all prayers.*

4

THE SOUL, PART TWO

The Twelve Attributes of the Soul

As we move through our human experience, we tend to construct a variety of mental and emotional barriers that prevent us from clearly knowing who we really are. It is time to lift the veil of illusion and dissolve those artificial barriers. It is important to remember that the external world is always a reflection of perceived inner reality. As inner perception becomes more refined, there is an expanded clarity of purpose and meaning to one's outer experience. You begin to see outer expressions that correlate to feelings that come from somewhere deep within.

We often find it difficult to identify the source of these feelings as there seems to be a cloud of forgetfulness shrouding the consciousness of the soul. At some point on the inner journey, it is discovered that these feelings resident within the soul reflect certain qualities that have a universal application in all cultures independent of language. These qualitative statements of existence are part of the core consciousness of every soul; they are called the Attributes of the Soul.[15]

The process of awakening is stimulated as you become aware of the rhythm of the flow of creation. Through repeated experiences over many lifetimes, you discover that the Attributes of the Soul

---

[15] *See Appendix E for a listing of the Attributes of the Soul and their numerical equivalencies.*

reflect the Attributes of Creation. That which is created has within it the essence and characteristics of that which creates. For instance, the sculptor's feelings and expressions are within the qualitative statement of the figure that is created from an otherwise undefined block of marble. Similarly, the painter's vision and awareness is captured in the form, color and shape presented on the canvas. Whatever you create has your inner feelings and vision imbedded in the created pattern whether in words such as in a presentation, poem or book, or in an objet d'art, a construction project, or the interior design of your home. The soul is no different. The soul was created as a spark of the divine Consciousness of Creation and has within its core consciousness all the qualities of the creative process.

There are twelve Attributes of the Soul. There are perhaps other attributes that can be identified but these twelve embody the fundamental eternal qualities of the creative process. The attributes are knowable, immutable, unchangeable, absolute, eternal aspects of the essence of the soul. They are the connecting link, the window to understanding and knowing the oneness of the soul with all creation.

Each attribute can be inwardly validated when deeply felt and then observed as an outer characteristic. For instance, we often have feelings of *beauty*, a qualitative statement of an outer observation. We say of a sunset, *that is really beautiful*. Where does the concept or feeling of beauty come from? Beauty is one of the attributes that resonates with a universal inner statement of *beauty* that can only be what it is. Likewise, we have a sense of *harmony*, an outer resonance in relationships, art, and music that we identify with because of the inner reality of a universal statement of harmony that can only be what it is. Beauty can only be beauty; harmony can only be harmony.

A common occurrence for every soul is that through

experiencing the opposite of a particular attribute, the meaning of that attribute is revealed. For instance, through stimulating discord, one learns the value of *harmony*. Through creating illusions of comfort and holding on to images of assumed importance, one learns the true meaning of *reality*. Through becoming attached to limiting ideas, dogmas and concepts of the three-dimensional world, one is eventually exposed to *truth*. Through living in a reactive, emotional way one learns the value of *balance* in life. Do any of these or similar situations sound familiar? Throughout our life experience, we are always facing the potential for an ever-deeper understanding of the Attributes of the Soul.

The true understanding of the attributes comes only through application. In every event, every relationship, in every aspect of daily life, the opportunity exists to apply what you know. *It is what you do, not what you think about, know, or intend to do, that counts.*

Every element of creation has an energy pattern radiating from core components. Energy patterns in the three-dimensional world have been explored and investigated for many years, most notably through the work of Georg Christoph Lichtenberg (1742-1799, experimental physics), Nikola Tesla (1856-1943, electromagnetism, wireless communication), and Seymon Kirlian (1898-1978, electricity, photography). Each of these scientists contributed greatly to the understanding of the unseen forces at work in energy patterns of the physical world. Currently research is being conducted utilizing the Gas Discharge Visualization technique (GDV) invented by Dr. Konstantin Korotkov, a leading scientist from St. Petersburg, Russia. This new technology allows a special computer driven camera to capture the physical, emotional, mental and spiritual energy emanating to and from an individual, plants, liquids, powders, and inanimate objects. This results in real-time viewing of the human energy field, or aura, with the potential for use in various healing modalities. The importance of the collective work of these and others is seen in the activities of the International Society for the Study of Subtle Energies and Energy Medicine (ISSSEEM) founded in 1989.[16]

Composed of a finer substance than the three-dimensional world explored by science, the soul also consists of certain energy patterns with identifiable qualities and attributes. This energy, or consciousness, has an external component reflected in the experiences of each lifetime, and an eternal inner pattern that is absolute. Remember consciousness is energy; soul energy is soul consciousness. The external energy pattern reflects the soul's emerging understanding of its true character and nature. This understanding, though limited in depth and perception, creates one's *assumed reality.*

Most of humanity dwells in this limited reality. The inner truth of one's true character and nature lies dormant, waiting to be discovered and remembered. Eventually, the soul stirs and begins to recognize the internal component of soul energy that defines the eternal nature of the soul. Within the inner energy pattern there is a rhythm of the universe reflected in the Attributes of the Soul. As the consciousness of the soul is awakened, expressing the qualities of the attributes becomes a moment-by-moment living reality, not a vague, philosophical possibility. The *eternal reality,* not the *assumed reality,* becomes the fully embodied expression of the awakened soul.

The Attributes of the Soul reflect the *eternal reality* of soul consciousness. One understands the attributes by observing the correlation between the soul qualities reflected in various attributes,

---

[16] *ISSSEEM is an international non-profit interdisciplinary organization dedicated to exploring and applying subtle energies as they relate to the experience of consciousness, healing, and human potential.*

and the energy of numbers and their universal application. Much has been revealed and written on the science of numbers, numerology, or esoteric relationships of numbers to various patterns of creation. When we study the Attributes of the Soul, we are in a way looking at the numerology of the soul. Each of the attributes when decoded resonates numerically to a corresponding number, one through twelve. These are absolute, immutable, unchangeable relationships that are the essence of the building blocks of soul reality aligned with the complete statement of the creative principle imbedded in soul consciousness. A full and complete understanding of these twelve attributes with total integration into all that a soul experiences leads to the capstone of Soul Consciousness reflected in the number thirteen.

You might be asking, *what is the value to know about these soul attributes? How does it apply to me, now, in this lifetime?* The answer is very simple. By understanding the Attributes of the Soul, you discover the underlying makeup of the soul. You discover the qualitative foundation of creation as revealed through the soul. It is like reading a blueprint that reveals how all is connected, all is one.

Each soul comes into a given lifetime with a purpose or destiny to be fulfilled. The destiny is not usually clear or evident but there is often a deep-seated feeling of purpose waiting to be revealed. Your destiny path for the current lifetime can be discovered from the perspective of the Attributes of the Soul. Underlying every lifetime is the soul intention to perfect understanding of certain attributes. This eventually leads toward a fully conscious realization of all twelve attributes.[17]

On a practical note, by knowing and being the conscious embodiment of the attributes, you walk through life seeing and

----

[17] *See Appendix F for a discussion of Finding your Destiny Path.*

knowing life for what it is. You are simultaneously the conscious observer and an active participant in the life process. Life is lived effortlessly for you know who you really are. You walk the pathway of harmony and peace, knowing truth, emanating love and light at all times! You came into this lifetime to remember and be who you really are. As you awaken to soul consciousness, the attributes become a living reality of every facet of your life.

It is like researching how a tree grows. By understanding the relationship between the earth, the weather, the root system, the physical makeup of the trunk, the process for emerging leaves and new growth, and then the process of photosynthesis, the tree can be understood. Its place in the scheme of things and how it relates to all other elements of the forest can be known. So it is with the makeup of the soul. When you know the attributes, you become the living embodiment of the qualitative essence of creation.

The twelve attributes of the soul offer doorways to a greater understanding of who you are. Each attribute has its own harmonic vibration. Each attribute has a unique quality that offers a perspective to the makeup of the soul. Each attribute is a symbol that reflects a composite statement of creation that is in harmony with the entirety of your being.

So as you go through the cycle of awakening, absorb, integrate and know the truth of each attribute. Each attribute is like a leg under the table of awakened consciousness. The table can only stand and be level and complete when each leg is in place. Feel the essence of each attribute. Integrate that essence into the greater understanding of who you are as you bring all twelve attributes into focus.

Attributes of the Soul, 1-6
Following is a discussion of each of the attributes and their

inherent meaning from a soul point of view. It might be helpful to meditate on what is offered and ask for inner confirmation and clarification on what you think you understand. Exposure to these concepts of eternal soul realities will lead toward expanded awareness and integration of the mind, body, and soul.

Spirit (1)

Spirit is a word or concept often used to link human consciousness with the unseen dimension that we sense is there and sometimes even experience. It is a rare soul who has not felt there is something more to life than what is in the immediate experiential environment. Throughout a soul's journey on Earth, there has been a continual quest to discover what lies beyond and to somehow connect with what is of an eternal nature. The concept of spirit is very comforting as we reach beyond our immediate grasp. As Robert Browning stated in his poem, Andres del Sarto, *Ah, but a man's reach should exceed his grasp, or what's a heaven for?* We do indeed reach into spirit for the meaning of life. From the soul perspective, spirit is identified with the very Source of all creation.

Spirit is the flow of energy that brings all things into creation. It is through spirit that form is created. Spirit is the animating force behind all of life. Spirit is formless, unseen, and infinite. Spirit is a statement of the divine in all dimensions of consciousness. Spirit is the spark that ignites the soul on its journey of experience and discovery. Spirit is love flowing through light into life. Spirit is the foundation upon which all other soul attributes are based.

Spirit is a difficult word to describe for it is really symbolic of all that exists. It is symbolic of the connectedness of all that exists in the created experience. It is the feeling, the flow of energy that forms a link in consciousness with the oneness of creation. Spirit is felt and seen in all aspects of manifestation. Spirit reveals a feeling of purpose and direction, and a feeling that something more lies beyond the immediate experience. Spirit reveals that the soul is one with all creation. Spirit flows in and through the soul releasing the eternal qualities of the Attributes of the Soul. Spirit is a most important concept to understand and, more importantly, to feel, and, even more importantly, *to be one with.*

Beauty (2) and Balance (2)

Spirit divides into two rays, beauty and balance, as the process of creation continues. These rays are parallel and equal and express a statement of the creative energy of the universe. In its purity of expression, the soul is imbued with beauty as a fundamental component or building block of consciousness. We see beauty all around us as we observe nature, the animal, plant, and mineral kingdoms, and particularly as we deeply observe another soul. Beauty is a natural state of the soul, a state of spirit expressing and knowing itself as the creative energy of the universe.

Beauty is also represented by the attribute of balance. This is a very important concept, for throughout all experience, we find that a natural condition of existence is one of balance. As we observe nature, we see how all forms of life coexist in a grand plan of balanced relationships.

The same harmonious relationship exists when two souls relate in perfect balance. The path of a soul through many lifetimes of experience is one of finding balance. As one veers from the spiritual path because of ego desires, emotional reactions, or attachments to the physical aspects of life, there is always an adjustment. There is often an inclination from within to find that point of balance that is the natural state of the soul. The world is accepted for what it is as lessons are learned while not becoming attached to worldly things. One discovers an inner perspective of walking the middle road in balance with all creation. The path of awakening to soul consciousness is straight and narrow requiring an integration of beauty and balance into one's conscious application of energy.

In the world of matter, you can physically see and experience the concepts of beauty and balance in many ways. You are able to see and experience these attributes because of the reference point within the soul. If beauty and balance were not part of your inner qualitative makeup, you would not recognize these qualities in the world around you. Beauty and balance are a natural state of existence. When one walks in balance in the flow of life energy, it is very beautiful.

Might (3)

The power of creation can be seen in the concept of might. Might is the sustaining quality of the soul that consciously connects the soul with the infinite source of all creative energy. Might emerges as a trinity expressed in many different spiritual persuasions, often as the Father-Mother-Child, Brahma-Vishnu-Shiva or Osiris-Isis-Horus. Might is also expressed as the triangle, the most stable universal geometric form used in art, construction, and also in symbolic representations of spiritual understandings. The mightiness of creation is very real. The soul, in its purest form, is a statement of the trinity, the mightiness of creation where the masculine and feminine principles of the universe merge as one.

Might resonates to the number three and is creation in action. Might is the blending and coming together of the masculine, or outer expression of energy, with the feminine, or intuitive inner energy. The projecting and outgoing aspect of creation merges with the calming, nurturing, and feeling component of one's being. When the mightiness of masculine and feminine energies is realized, the child of that union is created, a combination of the two as one. This is creation in its purest sense, the mightiness of the forces of the universe coming together to bring forth new form, new thoughts, new ideas.

Throughout creation, there is always a balancing of the masculine and feminine forces. There is the feminine force in the earth that is the nurturing, balancing, harmonizing aspect of that which provides substance and sustenance to the children of the earth. Then there is the radiant power of the sun, the masculine force projecting light and energy into the earth. The result is a balancing of the two energies in a unified statement of creation. It is important to know that the attribute of might, representing the mightiness of creation is present within the soul

Harmony (4)

Harmony is a natural state of being. Everyone resonates to harmony on some level as there is a desire to find that place of inner contentment where there is a sense of peace and stability. We hunger for harmony in our relationships with others, in our business and social activities. We yearn to experience harmony and understand our place in the grand scheme of things.

All of nature is in a state of harmony. The soul is no different. Harmony is the foundation for every experience in life. Such harmonious interaction is dependent upon the degree to which a soul is consciously aware of its true nature. Harmony reflects the creative energy of love in motion. Harmony, as an Attribute of the Soul, is waiting patiently to be expressed in every thought, word, and action. It is the foundation stone of manifestation.

Harmony is a statement of naturally balanced conditions within the soul. When harmony is expressed, there is an emerging awareness and understanding of soul reality. Within the soul, there is a natural connectedness with all creation. Harmony is most important to understand and more important to live as one applies what one understands.

Life (5)

Life is the animating principle of creation. As discussed in chapter two, love is carried into manifestation on waves of light; life is the result. To understand life is to understand the process of creation. Life is the flow of infinite creative energy which when activated by the soul stimulates an eternal quest to discover who the soul really is.

The energy of life exists everywhere. Life is certainly evident throughout human experience. You see life activating every cell in the human body. Life is seen in the growth cycles of plants, trees, and various biological forms. Life is also seen in the mountains, the ocean, created forms that surround you, the clouds, and in the wind. Life is seen in the man-made creations that make up our cities, our industry, our art forms and crafts. Life is in every atom and cell of existence. The essence of life is in everything you observe, feel, and dream.

Life is an eternal reality realized by the awakening soul as it moves through experience after experience. Life is the creative principle in action, the animating energy of creation. As you observe your environment, you experience an abundance of life. The life force within the soul is the same energy that is at the core of all creation. Life is not a limited concept. It is an infinite flow of the Consciousness of Creation present in all creation on all dimensions. If the life force were to cease, all existence would cease. Life is the energizing principle of the embodied soul.

Truth (6)

To know truth is to be truth. In the consciousness of truth, there can never be duality, good and bad, true and false. All is seen to be part of the whole. Everything is connected and there is a reason for everything that happens. The reason for a particular event or relationship is not always evident to the conscious mind. However, from the eternal perspective of truth, the reason can be discerned. Each event in one's life contains the seed of a lesson to be learned as the truth of one's existence is revealed.

All souls enter into a given lifetime with a chosen life plan that provides an opportunity to refine their understanding and grow into greater alignment with their true self. As alignment occurs, you discover the truth of existence and the eternal nature of the soul. There can only be one truth; there cannot be several truths. Truth is the universal principle of freedom. It was once given *know the truth and the truth will set you free*. The mind asks, to be free from what? The answer is very simple - to be free from the misperception that the assumed reality of your life in the three-dimensional world is your truth. Freedom is the natural state of the soul. Freedom is knowing the truth of who and why you are and then fully living that truth with every thought, word, and action.

Knowing the truth of one's existence frees you from attachments to the physical, mental, and emotional world. You see the world for what it is without fear of losing anything. In discovering your true identity, you find everything. The illusion of the world dims in importance as illumination from within lights the pathway to the discovery of truth. Truth is freedom of the soul.

Truth is an absolute, pure statement of what is real and eternal. Truth is found deep within the soul as the soul identifies with who it is, how it came into creation, its purpose, and the truth of its relationship with itself and with other souls. In the external world of experience, there appear to be many truths. There are many false concepts that are an illusion and façade of what for a moment seems to be true. These concepts will, in time, be seen for the limited truth they represent. As you awaken to the consciousness of oneness, truth is instantly known and understood. Truth is simply truth. Truth is the ultimate statement of oneness, the statement of who you are as a soul.

Attributes of the Soul, 7-12

The first six Attributes of the Soul form the foundation for awakening to soul consciousness. They are present as the core reality of every soul. All souls are destined to discover their true spiritual nature as they progress through many lifetimes in the school of Earth. As the twelve Attributes of the Soul are discovered, experienced, and internally known, the stage is set for leading to the ultimate goal of awakening to soul consciousness.

As you awaken to the inner meaning of the Attributes of the Soul, you discover a natural connection between the various attributes. The attributes refer to eternal realities that describe the fundamental makeup of the soul. When application of the attributes becomes part of every thought, word, and action, you approach living in the fullness of soul consciousness. You are conscious of who and why you are. You are consciously one with creation and with all other souls. The next six attributes along with the first six define the character and nature of the soul. When the twelve attributes are fully integrated into one's consciousness as an applied, living reality, there is a merging into the thirteenth attribute, which is the fullness of soul consciousness.

Intelligence (7)

Intelligence expresses the capacity to know, and know that you know truth. Intelligence is a filter and interpreter. Intelligence of the soul sees through, around, and behind all that is being expressed in the earthly experience, interpreting and bringing into greater understanding that which is being observed.

Intelligence is more than analyzing situations and making right decisions. It is more than the ability to figure things out. Intelligence is the capacity to interpret and apply universal truth in every aspect of existence. It is the conscious omni-dimensional awareness of a soul linking the gap between experience and reality. Human intelligence, an extension of the intelligence of the soul, is often restricted or restrained, often held back by attachment to what is being observed, analyzed, or responded to by the ego. Human intelligence is an indicator in the external environment of a greater capacity in the inner realm for intelligence of the soul to be fully realized. The function of intelligence is to bring the attributes into harmonious interaction, enabling you to live in the fullness of your true character and nature.

Image (8)
Image resonates to the symbol (8), which is essentially two circles, one over the other. The circle represents wholeness, the totality of creation, and the completeness of the soul. All that the soul is, all that the Consciousness of Creation is, is contained within the circle. So the two circles, one over the other, indicate the infinity of creation, whole and complete in both the outer and the inner form. The image of the Consciousness of Creation is implanted within the soul as a pattern of expression of all that the soul can express and manifest. The seen and the unseen, inner and outer reality, as above so below, are all represented in the symbol 8. From this perspective, a soul is able to understand the world in which it lives. Remember, the soul is the Consciousness of Creation in motion.

It is interesting to note that the symbol for infinity is eight (8) laid on its side (∞). This is the ultimate statement of the harmony of all creation where the Consciousness of Creation is in perfect balance with that which is created. Both are contained in the circle, joined together to form the symbol for infinity at the boundary between the manifested and the unmanifested.

Reality (9)

The number nine is a complete number. It represents the integrated expression of the first eight numbers. When reality is fully manifested in the consciousness of the soul there is complete understanding and application of the first eight attributes. Through reality, the true spiritual identity of the soul can be known. Everything is connected. All is one.

In transiting the earth experience, there is a significant challenge to clearly understand what reality is from the inner spiritual perspective. The *assumed reality* of the outer world of duality, reaction, attachment and ego positioning has a very strong attraction. You often see the world only through emotional, mental, or physical relationships. You miss the hidden meanings and do not see the connectedness of things. Once you understand that you are a soul experiencing life on Earth for the purpose of gaining experience, you begin to see every activity, every encounter from the connectedness point of view. You begin to live in the reality of who and why you really are as a soul.

In reality, the illusory aspects of the outer world, the façade of ego, emotional interactions and attachments to physical aspects of creation are seen for exactly what they are. When you really know and understand reality, truth emerges and the illusions fade. You know you are a conscious soul, one with the Consciousness of Creation. Reality leaves no room for falsehood or misconceptions, no room for living or being other than exactly who you are.

Opulence (10)

Opulence represents the fullness of experiencing all the richness of creation as an awakened soul. There are also the riches of the world, but these are of man and pale in significance to the opulence of the soul as reflected in the fully awakened soul consciousness. The soul knows its oneness with creation.

Manifestation of opulence requires maintaining a purity of intent, motivation, and application in all that you experience. As has been said many times, spirit will not be mocked. Where there is a self-serving attitude or desire to satisfy personal greed, no matter how subtle, the doorway to truly realizing the opulence of the soul will not fully open. Of course, the door can always be opened when the intent and motivation are in alignment with the truth of one's being.

The opulence of creation is a magnificent reality, always present and available. It offers a sense of grandeur, a sense of quality that is beyond what is usually experienced. It offers a sense of infinite bounty and supply, a sense of radiance that is as sparkling as a basket full of diamonds. Opulence is all of these things. It is through the attribute of opulence that one is able to understand, identify, and appreciate the qualitative aspects of creation. The true consciousness of opulence comes from within.

Light (11)

Light is the energizing force of all of creation. It is through light that creation takes place. Have you ever wondered where light comes from and what light really is? Light is energy. It is love emanating as creative waves of infinite energy manifesting as life. Light is packets of energy that exist on all dimensions giving vitality to the continuous process of conscious creation. Light, the carrier wave of love, is the essence of life. Without light there would be no life. Without love, there would be no light. If light were not supporting the energy of life, what would happen? Creation would stop. It would be as though nothing ever happened. Remember *love-light-life* is the *trinity of creation*.

Light is within you, within every soul. Light is within every cell, every atom of creation. Light is the animating energy that provides the foundation for life, the environment in which you live and create. Light is creative energy in motion throughout the continuum of existence. When soul consciousness is awakened, the creative energy of light is known.

Feel the light of creation pulsating and radiating from your entire being. Feel it as the core energy of your existence. Feel light as a flow of love emanating from the very center of who you are. Feel the light as it surrounds, permeates, and radiates through every nook and cranny of your consciousness, every cell of your physical body, and every aspect of who you are as a soul. Light is the quality of the soul that gives energy to all the Attributes of the Soul as they become integrated as one. Never hesitate for a moment to let this light shine, to let it be recognized for what it is. This is who you are as a soul, a radiant spark of light manifesting as life, a statement of love in action.

Principle (12)

There is an operating principle that underlies all creation. When a soul awakens, the pattern of creation is understood, the process of manifestation is experienced and the oneness with all creation is known. In this awareness, the underlying foundation of creation is fully experienced and known. It is seen that there is a continuum of dimensions; there is an infinite variety of created forms and energy patterns. There are cycles that all souls go through to learn what is necessary in order to understand and know the operating principle, the cosmic formula of creation. When you know this underlying principle of creation, you then know how all of the Attributes of the Soul work together as a holistic concept. The operating principle of creation is absolute and never changing.

It is dynamic with an infinite flow of energy. It is purposeful with the outcome being a process of soul-discovery. You, as a soul, awaken and know who you really are as a spark of the Consciousness of Creation.

The operating principle is also a higher vibration of might. When you see the mightiness of creation in action in a coordinated and unified manner with all of the attributes expressed, you understand the operating principle of the universe. Soul consciousness becomes a living reality!

Conclusion

You as a soul are a composite of the twelve Attributes of the Soul. So, is it practical to know about these attributes and how they are applied in everyday life? Yes! It is only in the application of what you know that you truly grow in understanding as you integrate the attributes into every aspect of your life and realize the capstone attribute of soul consciousness.

Being aware of the Attributes of the Soul and how they are applied through conscious life experience is a catalyst to assist in the integration of mind, body, and spirit. Through the knowledge of the chosen pattern of application of an attribute, you can consciously know why certain conditions exist and can face them head on. There is assurance that through mastering the inner meaning of a particular attribute, you will be one step closer to the fullness of soul consciousness.

5
COMPLETING THE JOURNEY

The Call to Awaken

The call has gone out. People around the world are receiving the call to awaken and know what it means. They know that it is time to respond, not a time for procrastination. You most likely have received the inner call to awaken or you would not be reading this book! The call has indeed gone out to awaken the slumbering soul. It is time for those who respond to the call to recognize the dynamics of this era and to integrate consciously with the truth of who they are as a soul. Each of us is on an eternal journey. As we hear the call to awaken, we realize that this is a time for action.

For many centuries in the earthly school there have been those who knew that there was something of great significance beyond immediate tangible experience. There has often been an urge to discover and learn what is on the other side, what might be called omni-dimensional existence. This discovery process has often been stymied by power struggles and controlling influences of organizations and individuals who with limited understanding used fragments of revealed information to control the minds of inquiring souls. Those in power wanted to utilize concepts, symbols and dogma in support of their own limited benefit.

More than just being called, the awakening soul is challenged to do something with what it knows. Often we hear the inner message but fail to act. We lack confidence in what we know and find it easier to remain in the world of reacting to outer experience rather than responding to the inner call. It is much easier to say, *no, not now, not me, I'm not interested or ready.* One can simply ignore the inner impulse. The question is always present: when are you ready to forego attachment to worldly concerns and matters of ego and consciously turn within to discover *who* and *why* you are? Many are called to cross over this bridge; only a few make the conscious choice to commit to the inner journey.

So the question is if we have heard the inner call to awaken, what are we going to do about it? There appear to be many options, but the point is we have to do something; the call cannot be ignored. We can no longer sit and wait for the heavens to open and angels of love and mercy to come and provide solutions for our earthly challenges. It is time to recognize that the source for all solutions to understanding the journey of the soul lies within the consciousness of the soul. All that is needed to assist in the classroom of life emanates from the inner truth of who you are.

The call to complete the journey has always been buried deep within soul consciousness. This is neither a new nor recent phenomenon. History is full of stories about enlightened souls who have held the candle of inner light so that others could find their way through the darkness of humanhood. In certain traditions some of these souls have been called saints, or in other traditions, avatars, gurus, or master teachers. At this point in the history of Earth, the call to awaken has increased in volume and intensity. More and more people are feeling the inner urge to awaken to a greater truth than what they have found in worldly pursuits.

It is time to connect the dots on the mysterious hologram of life and see the resultant image in its wholeness, its perfection, and its infinite connectedness with all creation. It is time to remove the barriers of misperception, to take off the blinders that have restricted vision to a grand chasm of human activity, a narrow, deep channel of focus. It is time to fill in that chasm of illusion with understanding and bring the canyon floor up to the level of the surrounding horizon where the infinite landscape of consciousness can be viewed, experienced, and known.

The inner yearnings of the soul need to be acted upon. The flow of expanding consciousness throughout the world is, indeed, a wakeup call. Information is flowing freely as multiple portals of discovery are opening allowing for more in-depth understanding of what the journey of the soul is really all about. There are currently several thousand web sites offering insights to greater understanding about life. As you study, meditate and interpret what you read and feel, you will be motivated to observe and listen carefully to what is happening around you. You will develop increased sensitivity to interactions with others. You will feel the dynamics of life imbedded in every moment and begin to release all that has attracted and held your focus on old paradigms of relationships and existence.

Have you ever considered from a deep inner perspective the significance of this age and the extent of potential influence each of us has on the momentum and flow of awakening energy? Rather than becoming a recluse or giving up on the life process, we have the opportunity to fully understand what life is all about, and then to exist within the life process as an awakened, enlightened soul sharing and being love and light, living in harmony and peace. We are *to be in the world but not of it*, to be the awakened shining light of the soul living life enthusiastically and joyfully but not attached to the world.

There is much that happens in your life that is responded to, reported on, and reacted to from a physical, emotional, or mental perspective. There is even more occurring at the soul level as you respond to the momentum of increased awareness. There is an infinite flow of energy moving in and through the soul, dissolving the crust of resistance that has limited your perception and prevented your awakening to the truth of who you are.

The Ecology of the Soul

As you move in consciousness to the inner realm, it is obvious to the discerning inner eye that there is a pathway to follow, a pathway of release and letting go, a pathway of recognition and remembering, a pathway guiding and directing one's awareness toward the pinnacle of the consciousness of oneness.

The metaphor of climbing the sacred mountain is often used as a symbol of the inner search. The pathway up the sacred mountain moves through a myriad of adventures formed in part by what has been carried forward with the consciousness of the soul from lifetime to lifetime. It is as though these previous life experiences need to be readdressed. They need to be understood and then dissolved from any attachment or residual impressions other than the lessons learned through each experience. As the pathway up the metaphorical mountain is followed, one ascends in understanding and awareness. The inner doorway of awakened consciousness opens wider as one proceeds with purpose, clarity of intent, with understanding and enthusiasm.

Climbing the sacred mountain follows the path through the jungle of human experience and then elevates one in consciousness above the canopy that covers the worldly activities. The penetration of this canopy makes one aware of what lies within the worldly experience. Upon arriving at the peak of the sacred mountain of consciousness, one sees the world for what it is. There is no longer a need for a reaction or response to the world. There is no longer attachment to what has been experienced and released and now lies at the foot of the mountain.

From this pinnacle of consciousness, one sees the beauty and harmony of the infinite abundance and bountiful supply of creation. There is a release of all that is no longer necessary, all that is part of the created life pattern that has brought the awakened consciousness to this pinnacle of awareness.

It is important to know that this pathway up the sacred mountain is attainable. This is not a metaphor accessible to only a few. It is your inner sacred mountain. The pathway you are on is leading in a focused and deliberate manner toward arriving at the pinnacle of oneness atop the sacred mountain of consciousness. There are many souls embodied on Earth at this time who are aware of this inner journey and are approaching the summit. There is a reunion of awakened souls taking place, a reuniting, remembering that all is one. As you walk the inner pathway, know that you are climbing the sacred mountain of oneness, the same sacred mountain that is being climbed and attained by many souls throughout the world. Everything is connected.[18]

You begin to recognize that there is a thread of connectivity between all points of consciousness. This is certainly seen in nature when you walk through a forest, along a stream, on a beach at the ocean, or just wander through your garden. As you look through the lens of connectivity you see that all parts of the system you are observing are connected. This connectivity is becoming more clearly understood by many through the study of ecology which basically acknowledges the oneness and connectedness of all aspects of creation. Nothing stands alone; everything depends on and is connected to other parts of the web of the ecological system.

So it is with the ecology of the soul. As the soul awakens and becomes aware of who and why it is, there is then an understanding of how the consciousness of the soul is connected to and one with all that exists. You know you are one with other embodied souls, with nature, with all life forms, and with all

---

[18] *For an example of the inner pathway, see Siddhartha by Hermann Hesse, 1922.*

elements of creation.

Along the journey of the soul, you begin to remember that you have always been connected to and one with the Consciousness of Creation. A good analogy is to consider the Consciousness of Creation as an infinite ocean. You, as a soul, are like a molecule or singular drop of the ocean water. You and all other individual drops are connected to each other and to the entire ocean. You each have all the characteristics of the ocean imbedded within who you are. On the journey of the soul, you are remembering this connection and inner reality. All is one, all is connected.

There is never a time when that which is created is separate from that which creates. In the same sense, as you create with every thought, word, and action you project, you are connected to every part of your creation. This should give pause for reflection to consider how many words you use daily. Consider emotions, feelings and thoughts you project. Consider action you take within your environment or with others.

You see, there are many ways where you are constantly projecting, constantly creating. You are never disconnected from that which you create. So it is most important to be conscious of what you are creating, aware of the creative impulse flowing in and through your awareness. As you awaken to who you really are, you consciously move into a space of creating harmony, beauty and peace. You stop reacting to the emotional environment that usually demands a conditional response. You see the world for what it is, a classroom with challenging lessons to be learned. As you face and learn the lessons, the journey of the soul becomes effortless, enjoyable, understood and meaningful.

Why not consciously create your environment so that it reflects the truth of who you are? You will begin to see a change. You will see a transformation of your environment, a shift in what is attracted to you and what you are attracted to. You will see a shift in who you associate with and you will see how they respond to the love and light you are consistently radiating. You create everything in your environment. You create the intersections between you and others. You create feelings that you have and responses to your environment. You then master the *trinity of human endeavor*. You realize that all creation is based on the foundation of love and light.

On the journey of the soul, it is most important to be aware of what you are focusing on. Consider what you are giving attention to for you create whatever is consistent with your intention. It has been said that everything begins with an intention. Be clear in your intentions to the point of being able to state your intentions any moment of any day. As you are pure and clear in your intentions, creative energy of the soul then fulfills those intentions as you move along the journey.

As always, it is up to you. Are you going to create what the world wants you to create, what the world is demanding from you? Or, are you going to create what is prompted from inner intentions of the soul? This may sound like an easy choice but it is often difficult to fulfill for there is much that is tantalizing, interesting and challenging connected with the created world. You will always use the outer tools of creation regardless of whether the creative impulse comes from within or is stimulated by external conditions. The goal, however, is to consciously create. Conscious creation is a process that requires diligence, attention to detail, attention to the flow of energy from within. It requires a conscious decision to fulfill intentions you have established for your current lifetime and current moment of existence.

Intent-Motivation-Application

As with so many aspects of our three-dimensional existence, there is another trinity that applies to consciously creating: *intent, motivation,* and *application.*

A key characteristic of this trinity is having the purity of intent to explore, to listen, to feel and to express what is revealed from within in an unbiased, unfiltered and focused manner. Pure intentions are for the highest good of all concerned and are based on expressing love and light rather than for satisfying ego or material desires. To move a pure intention into the world requires pure motivation to consciously create from the perspective of inner revelation not from the perspective of the world.

Much of what occurs in your experience comes down to application. What are you doing? How are you doing it? How does it relate to your journey of the soul? How does it integrate with all other aspects of the flow of consciousness?

It is important to be conscious of how every thought, every word, and every action is consistent, or perhaps not always consistent, with the flow of harmony, peace, love and light. You can grade yourself on how you are doing. You know when you are on a tangential path, perhaps feeling a sense of anxiety or fear, a sense of anger or disharmony about whatever the outer conditional activities might be. You also know, and know that you know, when you are in the absolute flow of love, light, harmony and peace. One needs to be aware, be alert, and be awakened to this flow of consciousness and then act in accordance with an inner intention to walk the pathway of being the embodiment of love and light.

Application is the doing, the process of acting on the motivation that is guided by intent. This is often where a stumbling block occurs. Doing something in support of the intentional process of being a conscious soul often becomes confused with doing something to satisfy the mind, emotions or ego. This shift of focus is very subtle. It is in the purity of application that the process of awakening gains great momentum. The purity of application completes the trinity and reinforces the purity of intention that has been motivated to be expressed as the awakening process expands and is sustained.

It is in the application of what you know where the rubber hits the road. It is where what is revealed from within is presented to the world and then remembered by the soul. As you act, you remember; as you remember you act.

Part of remembering is remaining centered, a term that is often used by those on the spiritual path. For some, being centered simply means putting one's emotions and mind in neutral and going within to a place of peace and harmony. This is a natural state of being that allows for the creative impulse and intuition of the soul to be clearly felt and heard. Being centered means remembering and being aware of who you really are while at the same time interacting in the world. On the journey of the soul you are constantly walking the middle road knowing the inner reality of who you really are while participating in the temporary reality of the outer world. There is always a choice of where to place your attention.

It is important to be aware of each step along the pathway of awakening. This means being conscious of not only what you are doing, but more importantly, why you are doing it. It means being conscious of what you say and why you say it, what you think and why you are thinking certain things. This all begins to make sense and to resonate with a way of life when the purity of intention, the purity of motivation, and the purity of application are consistently aligned with the inner truth of who you are. In this alignment, recognizing, knowing and being the truth becomes a clear potential. In an instant of recognition the soul remembers and the awakening process is accelerated.

Blueprint of Awakening

Completing the journey of the soul demands consistency in identifying what is real and eternal, and then applying what is stimulated and revealed from within. There needs to be consistency of being the truth you are, of being love, radiating light, and living in harmony, balance and peace. This is the blueprint for the awakening process.

Within the consciousness of the soul there is a blueprint, a plan, an expression of awareness waiting to be presented to the world. The blueprint contains the reality of who you are. As you release attachments, reactions and identity with the created world, you come into alignment with that blueprint. You live what is revealed and express the truth of who you are.

The soul appears to have a personality that is unique which is of course true from the outer perspective. There is a unique presentation being made in the world by each of us. This is as it should be, for we are all on our own journey working through a self-designed lesson plan, responding and reacting to life, becoming involved moment-by-moment with the environment we create, constantly learning and remembering.

The soul personality is a statement of outer conditioning you have created in order to move through the lesson plan for this lifetime. When the focus of the journey is turned within, inner exploration becomes the conscious intention of the soul. There is then an unfolding of the blueprint as waves of love and light rise to the surface of awareness and dissolve outer conditioning that has created the external personality, much as the flame of a candle melts the outer form and leaves only light.

As the blueprint unfolds, you begin to live as an example with the conscious application of love and light becoming the preferred pathway of expression. The true personality of the soul is then revealed; love and light are enthusiastically expressed with every thought, word, and action. There is clarity of vision as the soul knows who and why it is.

The soul's journey will always take you inward where the true pathway of life is unveiled and known. You have traveled this pathway for many lifetimes. Your soul experiences have been retained in what might be called the inner book of the soul, or the Book of Wisdom. All that you know as a soul is contained within this book. Over many lifetimes, you have developed increasing awareness of your purpose as a soul. This awareness has blossomed into full understanding and knowing, and has created the inner Book of Wisdom.

As you complete the journey of the soul, you need go no further than this singular point of inner awareness, the Book of Wisdom. There is no need to continue to strive to become more than you already are. There is no need to rely upon external emotions that pull you into limited aspects of fulfilling outer desires. These are temporary stopping places, not the goal or the ultimate pathway that you as a soul are discovering.

The ultimate pathway along the journey of the soul leads you to the Book of Wisdom. As you symbolically turn the pages of this book, you discover that you, as a soul, are complete. You have always been all that you can be. There is nothing lacking, nothing to be added to who you are as a soul. You have forgotten your connection to the Consciousness of Creation and are on a pathway of remembering, of reconnecting. There's a good chance that over lifetimes of worldly experience your vision has become clouded so questioning continues. As answers are revealed, you make choices, refine your intentions and act. You begin to remember as the journey of awakening continues.

6

THE DAWN OF AWAKENING

We are living in an era of dynamic change. There has always been change but we are now seeing change on a massive, global scale that has never happened before in recorded history. The economic systems of the world are being realigned and adjusted to new realities. Political systems based on power and greed are being challenged in many countries. We see the application of spiritual principles being applied in business and personal decision-making. We see an increasing volume of books on spiritual and metaphysical subjects. We see a merging of science and spirituality. Traditional religious practices are being challenged as questions are raised about their restrictive dogmas and traditions and their relevancy in today's world. We see a proliferation of spiritually-oriented information on the internet offering a wide range of insights about spirituality and the awakening process.

All evidence points clearly to an increasing momentum of awakening to soul consciousness throughout the world. The fact that you are reading this book testifies to the reality of that momentum! People around the world are recognizing their commonality with each other, how they are more the same than different. They are beginning to feel that *there is really only one process of creation, not yours and mine*.

Everything is being challenged. Nothing of the world as we have known it is left untouched. It is a time of shifting energy, and also a time of potential positive adjustment to a new reality for the era we are entering. We need to look at what we have assumed to be our reality and let go of limited false beliefs of power, greed, control, fear of lack of supply and abundance, and attachment to worldly emotions and substance. These and other belief systems have held us in bondage long enough. It is time to awaken to our true character and nature; it is time to remember who we really are.

The process of awakening to the truth of who you are as a soul is the greatest gift you can give yourself as you transit the earth experience. Realizing and receiving this gift is your fundamental purpose for this lifetime. As awakening occurs, you become increasingly aware of the infinite expanse of inner consciousness. You awaken to the inner reality of being a spark of the Consciousness of Creation. You begin to see the potential for far-reaching relationships of peace and harmony.

It is important to focus on what the process of awakening really is, and the manifestations that bring momentum to achieving this goal. You begin to feel the potential for there being a level of transcendental reality. You begin to see how every thought, every word, every action, every feeling, and all that is experienced in the earth environment is connected.

It seems reasonable to accept the concept of being a *soul with a body*. As we read spiritually inspired literature of past centuries, digest the history of the development of various religions, and explore metaphysical books that crowd the bookshelves of any modern bookstore, we see a common thread of searching and seeking always present. There is an emerging theme of discovering the reality of the inner you, the *I AM consciousness, universal mind*, the *real self,* the *real you,* or the *inner light.* The arrows of self-discovery all point within where the ultimate link with the infinite (God, Allah, the Consciousness of Creation, or whatever is the highest name you hold) can be made while still in the world and still in the body. To awaken to the truth of who you really are is the natural, driving force of existence.

We have all searched for this connecting link, sometimes consciously, always subconsciously. Humankind seems compelled to discover its relationship with the root source of creation searching through whatever window of potential is offered in the human experience. This unquenchable thirst for knowing the truth of existence emanates from the soul. It must be remembered that the soul is complete; nothing can be added to or taken away from the soul. You, as a soul, are a unique spark of infinite love and light emanating from the Consciousness of Creation. Through many lifetimes of experience you became attached to what was created and, to a degree, forgot your spiritual identity. The classroom of life has provided the environment to remember who and why you are as a soul. This is the *real* purpose for your journey through this life experience.

Mastery of Self

There is always an awakening process taking place. Often it is subtle and not consciously realized. At other times, the awakening process is consciously realized and is part of the intent of the soul to become attuned to the greater reality of who and why the soul exists, and who the soul really is.

The awakening process brings into focus all that the soul is challenged with as it passes through the life experience. The process of awakening is often called the mastery of self. What this implies is the soul awakening to a true understanding of the process of creation, the process of being a soul embodied, and the process of becoming consciously one with all that exists.

Mastery of self is an interesting notion to consider, for what is the self? The self that you often refer to is the part of you involved in the physical, mental and emotional activities that define your life. Then there is the self-related to the unmanifested soul reality, the pinnacle of awakened consciousness that all souls are striving to attain. This is the *real self* or the *real you.*

When mastery of self is focused on as a pattern of moment-by-moment application, the physical, mental and emotional components of one's existence are seen for what they are, tools of creation. The result of using these tools is then understood from an awakened inner perspective.

The mastery of self lies in consciously living with purity of intent, motivation, and application, where the application is consistent with being the full and complete statement of the Consciousness of Creation within the soul experience. The mastery of self is the potential and ultimate goal of every embodied soul. The pathway to mastery requires the soul's full attention and focus on establishing inner purity of intention. In doing so, there is then mastery over the physical, mental and emotional aspects of existence. You are the master of your destiny of awakening to soul consciousness. This is your goal, this is your intention to live the life of mastery of self.

Window of Remembering

The urge to awaken is stimulated at different times for different people. Often there is a window of remembering still open early in life. Sometimes the window doesn't open until later in the life cycle, perhaps when stimulated by a challenging or dramatic life experience like death of a loved one, loss of a job, a divorce, or serious illness. Regardless, the soul is always looking for an opportunity to consciously explore the meaning of life. At a very deep level of awareness, we all want to awaken. When this yearning becomes a conscious intention, the window opens wide and the momentum propels us along the pathway of awakening.

Extended awareness in children often becomes clouded as the

experiences of adapting to the ways of the world influence the conscious mind. The capacity to remember one's purpose and soul identity is driven deep within as the relationships and events chosen for the current lifetime are experienced. There are many children being born in the world at this time, however, that seem to radiate an aware and knowing capacity. This often becomes quite noticeable at an early age. These children, referred to as *indigo* and *crystal children,* have been the topic of much discussion since the early 1980's.[19] These children bring a new energy that is transforming the planet around us. They are independent thinkers, agents of change, often have vivid imagination, and converse with complete, well-developed understanding of concepts and ideas. It is as though a generation of teachers is arriving to help take the earth and its inhabitants through this time of change and transition.

As life is experienced, the soul memory fades. The veil of illusion thickens. There comes a time, however, on everyone's pathway of experience when an *awakening* occurs. An *awakening* is when there is an opening to awareness beyond the mental and emotional limitations of your immediate experience. You go beyond the dogma of traditional and often restrictive concepts of religious and philosophical belief systems. You go beyond simply reading and intellectually approaching some vague distant notion of spirituality. You begin to awaken to the reality of who you really are as a conscious link emerges between inner awareness and the assumed reality of your three-dimensional existence. There is a time in every person's life, when this will occur. You remember that you are passing through the earth experience to awaken to the truth of who you really are.

––––––––––

[19] *See www.crystalinks.com/childrensic.html for a discussion of indigo and crystal children. There are several other web sites that discuss these children.*

We have shared that there is a natural tendency when going through the awakening process to become attached to concepts, philosophies, belief systems, and rituals. The form or image representing an idea is often held on to tightly until at some point another doorway opens that allows for release of concepts that have served their purpose. Attachments along the pathway should be seen as way-points, not end-points. There is always another step to take as the journey of awakening continues.

It is important to become aware that awakening is taking place or has the potential for taking place. It is beyond simply feeling that something is happening. It is beyond believing that something might happen. Rather, it is a time when there is a knowing, an *absolute knowing*, that you are indeed a spiritual being. You know that there is an eternal link in the soul that connects you with all creation. When you reach that point of knowing, an inner switch is turned on and you fully awaken to the truth of who you are.

Awakening is often initiated as one is exposed to various events, conditions, relationships, and activities that provide the necessary dynamics and environment. Often these points of learning are not immediately recognized as having such a grand purpose, but a seed is planted that will later grow into expanded understanding. Interactions that take place seem to have meaning, but it is not clear what the meaning is. As you begin to consciously awaken and are committed to continuing the awakening process, it is important that each event and relationship be observed from an inner perspective. What is occurring within the context of an event or relationship that is calling for a greater understanding? What is being learned that stimulates an awakening to eternal realities such as truth, harmony, balance, beauty, or love and light?

These and other questions need to be asked, for in every encounter in life there is a potential lesson to be learned. You eventually recognize that you are a soul, an eternal component of the creative process. This is a big and exciting step to take. You move from being consciously immersed and restrained in three-dimensional experience to being aware of and absorbed in universal awareness. It may surprise you, but this is the pathway that we are all on. Being on this pathway does not mean that a conscious decision has been made to awaken. It is always an individual choice, maybe in this lifetime, or if not, perhaps in the next. This is the pathway, however, of awakening that is potentially triggered by each and every learning experience.

As the sun rises daily and then disappears over the horizon, as the stars make their apparent nocturnal journey across the endless depths of the universe, one is reminded symbolically of the rhythm of the soul. The soul, too, is on a journey coming into the worldly environment and then passing across the horizon of consciousness only to return again in cycle after cycle to gain new experience and understandings. There is a continuous awakening taking place as the soul remembers who it really is.

One experience we all face at some time is the transition process called death. When this occurs, we come face to face with an understanding that we are temporarily embodied in an *earth suit* to experience what we call life. Perhaps you have had a friend or relative who has died. You have memories of a lifetime of interactions. You also know that at the time of death, the person you knew is no longer in the body. Something has changed. The energy, or soul, has moved on, made a transition into another dimension. You realize that the soul never was the body but had used the body to experience life. The awakening continues.

How Do I Awaken?

The process of awakening is readily understandable by the mind and the emotions for, as one would say, it makes sense. But the question often remains: how do I awaken? There is a lifelong process of education that is part of everyone's experience. There is the formal education of schooling, and then the education gained through life's experiences. The question to reflect upon is what is your intention? Do you want to consciously walk the pathway of awakening? Do you want to move beyond the sensual, emotional and intellectual adventure of the three-dimensional world? Do you want to discover the truth of who you really are? Until there is clarity of intention to consciously walk the inner pathway of awakening, additional lessons to be learned will be faced as you move through cycle after cycle of life experiences. Of course, even with a clear intention of awakening, you will still be facing lessons to refine understanding and accelerate the awakening process.

There is a process you go through as a commitment is made to walk the pathway of awakening. There is a beginning point when you recognize there is something beyond the physical, emotional, and mental world. Three-dimensional perceptions begin to be viewed as limitations and boundaries that separate *this side* from the *other side*. A deep desire rises to the surface of consciousness stimulating the exploration and desire to discover a greater meaning to life. Eventually through reading, sharing, and perhaps a dramatic spiritual experience, you discover that the pathway to soul-realization lies within the consciousness of who you are each moment of your existence. You begin to realize more clearly who you are as you focus on the emerging sense of connectedness welling up from within.

It becomes important to quiet the mind as the focus goes within. It is like putting your car in neutral, letting it idle, knowing the car is there, knowing there is energy flowing, but yet the car is still and unmoving. In the same manner, the mind, once it is quiet and put in neutral, no longer controls the process. It becomes simply a tool of creation, resting in the silence, waiting for the impulse from deep within the consciousness of the soul to stimulate creative action consistent with the soul's intention. *The mind is the servant of creation, not the master.*

It is also important to quiet the impulses coming from emotions and attachment to the physical world. These impulses are rather strong at times. They are the reactive elements of the human experience that respond to outer stimuli. Your emotions are like the litmus test of life ranging from completely passive to overtly reactive. The awakening soul will learn to use the outer emotions to reflect the inner emotions of the soul that respond with love and light to all events of life. The emotions are a doorway to the landscape of the soul reality.

As emotions are quieted and physical attachments are set aside, the mind is freed to respond only to the inner impulses from the soul. The process of opening the inner doorway to expanded consciousness occurs more easily. The awakening process is stimulated with a desire to proceed deeper into the discovery of inner realities in order to answer the question of *whc am I* and *why am I?*

The Age of Awakening

The age of awakening is a reality. The awakening soul feels a strong inner motivation to understand, to know, to move beyond words, intellectual discussions and philosophical musings. You want to know the truth. Partial truths or modified truths are no longer acceptable. The power structure of institutions and individuals who would control the flow of information and perceptions is no longer valid. You, as a soul, are awakening, unencumbered and free.

There is resistance by many to the awakening process and some of the new concepts that challenge old belief systems and understandings. There are those who do not easily accept new thoughts and ideas and are fearful of this transition to multi-dimensional reality. There are those who are curious as they observe various aspects of the awakening taking place but do not really understand. Then there are those who understand a little and thirst to know it all. And there are those who know the truth of who they are for there has been much preparation in the inner realm for this time of awakening; they will assist others in making the transition to the truth of their existence.

This is a time when it is most important to pay attention to the signs around you, to pay attention to the inner urges and nudges within you, to follow your intuition and listen very carefully for the voice of guidance that is always present as the awakening process unfolds.

This is an era of transformation. It is as though there has been a switch thrown and the world is being told to wake up. There is a shifting of focus as many are finding a spiritual path and are consciously or unconsciously awakening to an understanding that the transformational process they are going through is one of remembering who they are as an immortal soul. This process is occurring on a continual basis. There appear to be certain windows that open with instantaneous advances in understanding, all part of a process that has only one objective or purpose: the awakening of the soul.

All outer conditions are but passing symbols of the creative process that we have to some degree identified with. We live in an assumed reality twenty-four hours a day. We experience the environment around us using the tools of creation we are blessed with, namely the mind, senses, emotions and physical body. The soul is the eye of creation that is viewing, seeing and sensing all creation. The soul is on a journey of integrating understanding of the creative process into its purpose and intent for this lifetime.

The pinnacle of awakening is when we reflect love and light at all times, in all conditions, in all thought, all words, and all actions.

So embrace this transformational era enthusiastically and know that as you awaken, anxieties, fears, attachments and misperceptions simply disappear. They no longer have meaning. It is entirely up to you how quickly transformation occurs. But when the objective is clear, when the intent to awaken is consciously focused upon, the transformational process happens rapidly.

Awakening is a step-by-step process much like walking through a house, opening one door after another, exploring each room then going on to the next until the house is seen in its entirety. It is an integrated and gradual progression. The awakening process is a continuum where all the pieces of the puzzle of life and answers to innermost questions are revealed along the pathway of experience. The intent of the awakening soul is to first gain a glimpse of its eternal nature through life's experiences. As this is accomplished, the expanded intent to awaken is stimulated and activated.

You, as a soul, are part of the continuum of the creative experience. You have chosen to manifest in certain ways, leading to the exact point where you are now. You have come into a life pattern, are creating an environment around you and participating in certain earthly activities. You don't then just disappear and say that was that. You are part of an eternal continuity of life energy.

Each of us must rely on our own intuitive perceptions to discern what resonates deeply within. As you awaken, you remember that there is only one truth and filter out what doesn't fit. You take what is offered from various teachings and interpret what is necessary to understand the current lifetime. You begin to resonate with those concepts that remind you of who and why you are. As there are additional experiences, you begin to understand that you are on a pilgrimage, a journey of returning to awareness that you are a spark of the Consciousness of Creation. You remember your true character and nature, your true self. It is through this realization that awakening to soul consciousness becomes more than a philosophical possibility; it becomes a living reality: the *real you* awakens.

Once you begin to awaken and embark on a serious search for your roots and identity, there is no turning back. The flow of consciousness begins to accelerate and your yearning to rediscover your true self becomes the central focus of all life's activities. You realize you are transiting the earth experience to refine understanding, to experience what is necessary to cleanse and purify the mental, physical, and emotional bodies. In every experience you are simply facing yourself. In every situation, you can only see what you first see within yourself. Thus in every activity lies the seed of a learning experience that either consciously, or unconsciously, brings you face to face with your perception of reality.

The mirror of life is very accurate! To become aware that you are actually on a path toward understanding what life is all about is transformational. You experience an invigorating, motivating, and satisfying transition from being attached to the world to being committed to the inner search for truth. Your purpose and destiny in life become clear. The awakened soul is free from the influence of worldly attachments, free from emotional reactions to the flow of life energy, free to explore truth and to live life consciously attuned to being the love and light of creation. The journey continues. You know that the goal of awakening to soul consciousness is attainable and real.

7

THE FIVE STEPS TO AWAKENING

As suggested in the previous chapter, everyone at some point in their lifetime ponders the question of their existence and beyond that the existence of the entire universe. Who am I? What is this world and universe all about? Why am I here participating in this life activity? Have I had previous lifetimes on Earth? What happens when I die? Who am I, really?

Do we find answers to these questions? Do we eventually awaken to the truth of who we really are beyond the evidence of the physical, mental and emotional world? Perhaps we do, at least partially, as we become aware of inner feelings and revelations, and awaken to what it means to be an embodied soul. As we awaken to this fundamental truth, other aspects of our life journey begin to make sense. Previous chapters of this book have discussed what a soul is, the process of creation, the journey of the soul and the awakening process. Perhaps you have opened an inner doorway to a pathway of discovery that will lead to additional answers and help resolve the mystery of creation. That inner pathway is the pathway of awakening to soul consciousness.

As you proceed along the pathway of discovery, every time you speak a word, offer a thought, or take an action, the result is always the out-picturing of the consciousness known, felt and understood at that moment. Over your lifetime, you have put roots of potential deep into the inner recesses of consciousness. From time to time you connect with these roots tapping into the pure potential of love and light. You observe what comes forth in a variety of creative expressions. These roots go deep, ultimately to the Source, the Consciousness of Creation.

Over many life cycles, you have had experiences when the roots of awareness did not go very deep. They might have only gone to the emotional, mental or physical level. Your reaction to the created environment then reflected that level of awareness. Then there have been moments as you began to awaken where those roots have gone deeply to the very source of truth. As this has occurred, you have felt and expressed the wonder of walking in peace and harmony, and connecting with the infinite beauty of life.

Consciousness always flows from an inner perspective to outer awareness and application. As you observe your feelings and actions, you know how deep your root of connection is. You know when you are feeling and expressing love and living in harmony. You also know when you are not. When the latter occurs, perhaps it is time for deeper reflection to awaken more completely. It is time to observe your life patterns carefully and then reflect on the essence of truth revealed from within.

Going within is sometimes a vague and mysterious notion, for in our humanhood we often find it easier and more natural to identify with tangible, solid evidence of the life process. However, when the awakening begins to accelerate, we find that there is substance and meaning to the trail of discovery revealed from within.

This inner trail of discovery is really a continuum of experience with many components all leading toward expanding awareness. To assist in moving along this trail, there are certain points of focus that are helpful. These points are called *The Five Steps to Awakening* and can be adapted to your individual journey to fit your particular needs and commitment.

These steps represent an inner focus that expands the potential for awakening to soul consciousness. When one's intention and motivation is clear, participating in these five steps greatly accelerates the awakening process. It should be mentioned that these are not discrete steps like walking up a flight of stairs where each tread represents a specific level of progress. Rather they are descriptive of an inner process that is always present and active once you are committed to the pathway of awakening.

The five steps or phases of the process of awakening are:

Contemplation → *Meditation* → *Revelation* →
Illumination → *Enlightenment*

These words are used to bring focus to how energy, or consciousness, moves along the continuum of awakening. Words are subject to interpretation, they are not ultimately definitive. Feel what the words imply as you discover the meaning behind the meaning and become attuned to the inner sensitivities of the awakening process.

Contemplation

The first step is *contemplation*. Contemplation refers to a process of responding to an inner feeling that there is something lying just beyond the senses and impressions of tangible experience. You might have a momentary intuitive feeling that there is something greater and more inclusive of the magnificence of creation. You feel a ripple of consciousness that connects you to this expanded perception. This is the process of contemplation.

Being contemplative is a productive, stabilizing and harmonizing activity. Moments of contemplation generate an expanded sense of reality. For instance, when observing the moon as it rises in the night sky with its various tones and shades of color, something stirs deep within the soul. There is a sense of beauty, a feeling of grandeur, and an inner knowing that there is something beyond what is observed. Contemplating the moon evokes imagination and an appreciation for the infinite majesty of the observable universe. The moon and Earth are recognized as being one tiny component of seemingly infinite three-dimensional space. One is filled with feelings of peace, beauty, and a connectedness to life.

It is always important to consciously apply what you know to what you are currently experiencing. As you apply the expanded consciousness you have touched within, your outer experience becomes alive with a vitality that is contagious. You become an active, conscious participant in life sharing love, radiating light, exhibiting and being harmony and peace. Life is lived enthusiastically with anticipation of every moment being very precious. You walk and live a contemplative life applying what you know to be true every moment of your existence.

Contemplation brings forth a sense of awe and inspiration. A recommended contemplative process is to focus on an object of beauty such as a flower, the face of a loved one, a sunset, a vista or a mountain. Or perhaps your focus is on a pleasant thought, the aroma of incense, quiet musical tones, or a particular color. The process of contemplation leads to feeling the magic, beauty and mystery of life. We are always looking for the meaning behind the meaning.

As you walk the pathway of awakening to soul consciousness, live the contemplative life. Be aware of the magic of creation all around you and within you. Take a moment now and then to touch that inner connective link of consciousness and you will feel a sense of peace and harmony. You will feel the oneness that underlies all creation. You will be more aware and awakened as you move through life's activities.

Meditation

The consistent practice of contemplation leads one to the deeper inner practice of *meditation*. Through meditation you go beyond the feelings that come from contemplation. You enter into the silence where you move away from thoughts, feelings, or attachments to the world. The mind is stilled. It is in the silence where you begin to touch the core of who you are as a soul. It is in the silence that you receive guidance that moves you along the pathway of awakening.

For centuries, meditation has been a practice of numerous spiritual disciplines. Much has been written on the subject as it is the keystone of the awakening process. There are many approaches to meditation. They are all good, for each, in its own way, directs one's attention to the inner plane of consciousness. The practice of meditation leads you to connecting with the Higher Self, that part of you that is one with universal consciousness [20] It is not important which meditation process you use. The point is not to analyze but rather to be consistent in your commitment.

As you move into a meditative mode, it is always interesting to feel where the process leads for there are many gradations of awareness as the mind, body, and emotions are quieted. It is like climbing a mountain, going up through the forest above timberline, leaving the concrete, manufactured, human-created world behind as you move into the higher atmosphere. You soon reach the apex, the top of the mountain, where you view a seemingly infinite, boundless, limitless expanse. All is quiet, all is peaceful and calm. There is a sense of simply being.

Meditation is a process of alignment where the consciousness of the soul, once free from attachments, aligns with the truth that lies embedded deep within. Practice moving consciously into the

---

[20] *For a discussion of the Higher Self, see Appendix C.*

inner sanctuary of the silence and connecting with the truth of who you are as a soul. As you do so, you will feel and know that you are a soul in the body but you are not the body. You will feel love, you will feel light. You will feel life energy moving in and through every cell of your being. Consciously or subconsciously you are always in a process of inner alignment and awakening.

Remember, the form of the inner search or what you call it is not important. The point is to be committed to the process of meditation; the results will be self-evident. Meditation is the key to awakening to soul consciousness.

Revelation

During or following meditation, there is often a flow of awareness, or awakening energy, that rises to the surface. You experience *revelation*. There is sometimes a sudden *aha* as an answer comes to a question you have been pondering. Or perhaps there is a quantum leap in understanding the true character and nature of who you are. Revelation can also lead toward developing a deeper awareness of the creative process. Or there may be increased awareness about your purpose and destiny. Your destiny becomes clear when you are open and prepared to hear what is revealed and are committed to a path of spiritual discovery.

Illumination

Revelation leads to *illumination*. Illumination is like turning a rheostat that controls the flow of electricity to a light fixture. As the flow of electricity increases, there is more light. It is like walking into a dark room where you can move around and feel certain objects. You're not clear in your mind what it is you are doing or where you are, or what is happening, or what the objects are. But eventually you move forward and make contact with a switch which, like a rheostat, gradually increases light and understanding. You begin to see and interpret what you have been bumping into and stumbling over in the darkness of the room. As the light gets brighter, you begin to see more of the challenges you met in the darkness. You begin to see the relationship of the various objects. As the light gets even brighter, it becomes clear that there is a pathway through the maze of obstacles, or maze of experiences. You find that it is now easy to navigate through the room for you see it all clearly. The obstacles or potential experiences are not eliminated but you can easily move through and around the obstacles without having to be entangled in a web of reactions in the darkness of the room.

As you are consistent in your dedication and commitment to discovering the *real you*, there is increasing alignment with the flow of creative energy. You become aware of the infinite potential of the indwelling soul that you are. You feel the infinite love and light of creation. The awakening process gains great momentum as you walk through life as an illumined soul responding from an inner perspective rather than from an outer conditional response that is the way of the world.

Enlightenment

The capstone of the awakening process is when the soul reaches a state of *enlightenment*. The concept of enlightenment has been referred to rather extensively in various spiritual studies over the past hundreds and thousands of years. Enlightenment is a concept that is often held up as a goal for the aspiring soul. It is often misunderstood or, more correctly, not fully understood.

Enlightenment is part of the continuum of awakening as one approaches the consciousness of oneness. Oneness is the true center of soul consciousness coincidental with the core consciousness of all creation.

Enlightenment is a phase along the pathway of awakening

where a soul becomes fully aware of and one with the light of creation. When one is enlightened, they know not only the truth and reality of the worldly environment, but are also aware of the movement of love and light through many layers of creation. The soul understands the interrelating aspects of the creative flow of energy. The enlightened soul knows and activates truth in all of life's experience.

Being enlightened is not a statement of separation or of escape from the world. It is a statement of reality within the current lifetime where there is complete integration and application of the inner light of creation. Enlightenment is completion of the cycle of awakening.

The Awakened Soul

The awakened soul clearly sees a pathway through the multitude of challenges, obstacles, and other concerns in the worldly environment. Enlightenment is the apex of illumination, a goal and potential reality of awakening to soul consciousness. It must be remembered that the process of awakening is along an integrated and gradual continuum of progress. Certain terms are used to describe or explain the process. The answers to the question of *who and why am I* are revealed moment by moment along this continuum.

The awakened and enlightened soul moves through life with a radiance and glow of being love and light. The soul's aura expands infinitely out into the environment rather than simply being a limited aura of energetic activity on the mental, emotional, and ego-centered plane of existence.

Why not recognize and be the truth of who you are every moment of your life? When you next cross paths with a friend, relative, or even a stranger, feel your aura of love and light penetrating the physical and mental barriers of perception. Feel an embrace soul to soul. See the response reflected in the eyes and physical expressions of the other person and know that you have shared deeply the love and light you are.

It is impossible to describe in words what is infinite. It is only by going through the process of contemplation, meditation, revelation, and illumination, that a soul truly experiences enlightenment. The soul enters into a state of *knowing* that is beyond thought, beyond emotions, and beyond the physical. In some eastern traditions this state of enlightened awareness is called *samadhi, nirvana or moksha*. The enlightened soul is in complete unity with every aspect of existence; the enlightened soul is consciously one with the infinite expression of creation.

To arrive at this goal requires focus, a deep desire, and commitment. It also demands consistency. It requires application of love and light in every aspect of life. The doorway to soul consciousness is always open. Whether or not you walk through that doorway is up to you!

The only path to soul consciousness is through experience. You need to apply what you know in order to gain refinement of understanding. As you learn, you grow in awareness. As you grow in awareness, you refine your thoughts, your words, and your actions. Experience leads to understanding. Understanding leads to knowing. Knowing leads to illumination and illumination leads to enlightenment. Enlightenment is being conscious of who you are as a soul while simultaneously being both the observer and participant in life's activities.

The pathway to soul consciousness lies within the very experience you are having at any moment. Every moment of existence contains the opportunity to apply what you know. All souls are ultimately on the same path. As we apply what we know, we help each other awaken. Remember, all is one.

Meditate regularly. Allow the continuum of the five steps of awakening to be integrated into your life pattern. Feel the awakening momentum as you become clear on who you really are. We are each in our own way approaching the same goal of awakening to soul consciousness. Feel the web of awakened points of light spreading throughout the world.

Turn off worldly input of judgment, fear and greed. Let love and light permeate every aspect of your life. Be love consciously and consistently with family, friends, business and community. It is time to be released from the repetition of life cycles that have held you in bondage to the earthly experience. It is time to fulfill your destiny of awakening to soul consciousness!

8

AWAKENING TO SOUL CONSCIOUSNESS

Why Am I Here?

There is nothing more important than to awaken to the truth of who you are. Why else are you here? Some would say we're here to simply enjoy life, to participate in the infinite variety of life's experiences awaiting us each day. This is certainly part of the journey. But it seems there is always something pulling us deeper into questioning our existence. For centuries, philosophers and spiritual teachers have helped people discover, at least in part, answers to questions asked about the meaning of life. Ultimately, however, the inquiring mind comes back to the basic but profound question of *why am I here?*

When you ask this simple question, there is only one answer. You are here experiencing activities and events on Earth in order to awaken to the truth of who you are. Again, this does not mean that you avoid and walk away from or ignore life's experiences. It simply means that you awaken and see the world for what it is. You see relationships for what they are. You know that every person you encounter in life is on a path of awakening to the same ultimate truth. At some level of awareness they each have asked the same questions about life: *who am I* and *why am I here?* The answer is straightforward: you are here to awaken to soul consciousness. There is no other answer.

Once this answer is internalized, known and accepted, once awakening becomes the focus of your journey, everything you do will support and stimulate the awakening process. All that you think, say and do, all activities and projects you are involved in will reflect your awakened consciousness. You will radiate love and light as you move through life. You will walk a path of harmony, peace and balance. You will approach life with joy and enthusiasm experiencing life to the fullest, knowing what life is all about. You will respond rather than react to life. You will appreciate all aspects of creation, honoring all life. And, you will walk a pathway of love and service to others, for there is no higher calling for the awakened soul than to be and share love.

It is important to utilize correct terms and concepts when discussing the awakening process so that there is clear understanding of what is actually taking place as the soul awakens. There is indeed an awakening taking place where there is a realization, though often slow in developing, that the soul is complete as an immortal, eternal spark of the Consciousness of Creation.

There is often a perception that an evolution of consciousness is taking place as the soul, over time, awakens to its true identity. In the truest sense of soul reality there is no evolution taking place for the soul is already complete. There is simply an awakening to that which already is. This is an understanding that is very helpful as one moves through everyday experiences, for there appears to truly be an evolutionary process in the physical world. This process reflects the continuous impact of the movement of creative energy. Nothing ever stays the same. Evolution is another word for simply observing change.

Do you feel the winds of change blowing through each moment of your life experience? It is an awesome understanding to recognize that the continuous process that appears to be change is really just expanding awareness and awakening to soul consciousness. The outer appearance reflects what the soul understands and perceives at the moment. But the purity of soul consciousness never changes. Outer form and substance may vary, but the truth of who you are as a soul remains the same.

But what is this process leading toward? It is leading toward an awakened understanding that within the consciousness of the soul, there is no change, there is no evolution, the soul is complete, all is one. There is nothing for the soul to evolve into. You as a soul are an eternal, immortal radiant beam of the Consciousness of Creation. There is nothing to add to what you are as a soul. Your pathway through life is the process of awakening to soul reality. It is important to use the terms and understandings that provide the reference point for knowing that the soul is complete.

What is, simply is. That is the fundamental statement of the truth of soul reality. As creative energy flows through the lens of outer activity, the lens of emotional and physical interaction, the lens of the ego and mind, the creative patterns appear to vary in shape and substance. Remember, however, that the source of all creation remains constant. The creative process has an infinite, eternal foundation of the *Trinity of Creation* – love, light, and life flowing endlessly in and through all creation. So don't be misled or misguided by assuming that change is taking place within the soul. What is occurring is an evolution of awareness, an increased recognition of the oneness of the soul with all creation.

Classroom of Earth

Awakening to soul consciousness requires many cycles of experience in the classroom of Earth. In each life experience, there are events that lead to greater understanding. Often this process begins with questioning, wondering about life and the seemingly miraculous events that regularly occur. The soul continuously sends impulses to the open, inquiring mind as it yearns to be free, unencumbered by the false ideas it has carried forward through lifetimes of experience. The mind is an incredible tool of creation with the capacity to observe various aspects of creative activity and to analyze and intellectually correlate what is observed, expressed or heard. As the mind analyzes, you eventually understand and know that there is a deeper truth buried within the soul. But remember, the mind is the servant of creation, not the master.

It is through additional lessons in the classroom of life that misconceptions are released. You become aware of being *a soul in a body, not a body with a soul.* Each experience is like walking through a doorway of opportunity for inner discovery: one door closes, another door opens. There is always another door to walk through. The challenge is to recognize each doorway as a step along the path in the awakening process. Each new experience represents an opportunity to awaken. Each moment of awakening is like polishing a facet on the eternal diamond of truth and seeing more clearly the pure light of creation emanating from within.

The process of passing through these portals of awakening has two aspects. The first is letting go. With each new experience, it is incumbent upon one who is on the spiritual path to release and let go of what's behind the doorway that has closed. You have to release what has been held on to as a result of your worldly experiences. You need to release the habit of being in a reactionary environment with expectations of certain patterns to unfold. As these are released, the focus and attention of the soul is then open to what lies just beyond the next doorway.

The second aspect is accepting the potential for infinite possibilities of creation to be realized. As the next doorway opens, there is refinement and clarity of vision of your purpose and intent for this lifetime. Your pathway is clear and you act according to what is revealed from within. You see each experience as a stepping stone toward complete understanding of who you are, a step toward awakening to soul consciousness.

Life becomes an incredible, enlightening experience with each moment being like a brilliant star strung on a halo crowning one's consciousness, reflecting the inner light of the soul. You realize that within each precious moment lies the potential to fully awaken to the truth of your existence. Your perception of truth reflects the filters and conditions that are retained in the applied consciousness of the soul. It is important to recognize these filters, to see them for what they are. They are but passing kernels of observation. They are not permanent fixtures of soul reality.

Perceived truth comes in many guises. It is important to go beneath the surface of awareness, beyond misperceptions, to dissolve the barriers and boundaries that have been self-created to discover the one truth of existence. It is important to simply know the truth that you, as a soul, are a part of and one with the Consciousness of Creation.

Knowing this truth shifts focus from a worldly consciousness of duality and differences to an understanding of unity that is beyond the mind and intellect. It is clearly seen how all creation is connected. As you awaken to this understanding, you begin to observe life and all its variations in a more comprehensive manner. You know that the entire three-dimensional world is composed of energy – atoms, molecules, cells – all sustained by a single source of creative energy. This creative energy forms an infinite array of matter from the microcosm to the macrocosm. This creative impulse or energy called the Consciousness of Creation is omni-present, it is everywhere, in and as everything. This being true, we can see that all is connected, all is one.

Oneness

When we say all is one, we are referring to a concept called *oneness* which applies to the elements of creation as well as to all embodied souls. Oneness is more than just two souls thinking and acting alike, or having similar attitudes and understandings. Oneness is more than recognizing all souls as spiritual beings, though of course that is true. The full understanding of oneness is much deeper. Oneness is an infinite embrace of everything that exists. In many studies, the symbol of the circle is used to indicate oneness or everything that exists in all dimensions. Visualize the circle and then see the boundaries of the circle stretch out to infinity. Feel and sense the enormity of oneness where everything from the sub-atomic particles of matter to the outer boundaries of the universe and beyond is contained within the infinite boundaries of this circle.

As you ponder the concept of oneness, what do you feel? What do you sense? What do you know to be true? Oneness is not a passive concept. As you see the animated forms of life energy around you, as you feel the energy of love within you, it should be clear that the consciousness of oneness is active and all-encompassing. There is nothing, absolutely nothing apart from the consciousness of oneness. Awakening to this reality and truth of oneness is a major rung on the ladder of awakening to soul consciousness.

Oneness is not an intellectual or philosophical perception. We cannot discuss what oneness might or might not be. Oneness simply is. This is difficult for the mind to comprehend for the mind wants to divide, analyze, segment and categorize. The mind wants to see differences so it can manipulate and maneuver through the intellectual maze of thinking and then, by thinking, consider that it must therefore know. Oneness does not know differences or variables in lifestyles, patterns of behavior, belief systems, colors or other external characteristics. Oneness is within all these things, for oneness is simply the eternal all-inclusive statement of what is. All that you observe, see, and interact with in life, all that interacts with you, is from the same Source. *Everything is connected. All is one.*

When you awaken to soul consciousness, the concept of *one* becomes a reality. You are given many clues along the way. The question is, have your outer senses been opened to accept and understand that we are all *one*? It is time to realign with oneness as you discover *who* and *why* you are as a soul. As this takes place, you respond to the call that has gone out to awaken. You recognize the oneness of all embodied souls and all creation, and know that we are each on the pathway of awakening whether consciously recognized or not!

Soul Identity

Awakening unlocks the identity of the soul. The mind, the ego, the emotions fade into the background becoming part of the panorama of creation but not the driving force or the controlling energy. When the identity of the soul is viewed from an awakened inner perspective, you see a beautiful, homogeneous, and brilliant statement of the creative principle of the universe manifesting and expressing.

The soul is the main channel of expression for the flow of creative consciousness. It is through the soul that the creative process is known, appreciated, identified with, and then integrated into an understanding of oneness. It is only through the soul that such awareness is possible. Doesn't that give you an expanded sense of the significance of who you are as a soul? As you awaken, you begin to understand how all is truly connected. You simply know and express truth.

Every embodied soul is on a journey that has signposts along the way. There is scenery of a landscape of experiences, and more than that an inner arrow pointing toward a destination. The destination is not a place, a singular belief system or concept of existence. The destination is awakening to the reality of who you are as a soul, an infinite expression of love and light. You are going through many experiences in life discovering, remembering, and awakening.

Some of the signposts point to accomplishments and periods of awakening. Everything has a temporal aspect, a temporary concept of reality. One should not hold on to or give undue attention or importance to these manifested points of creation. They are there to stimulate a greater inner understanding. Some signposts involve other people you encounter, events and activities, sudden revelations and other observations. Know that every moment is very precious for contained within every moment of your experience is the potential for opening ever wider the inner doorway of awakening.

Awakening to soul consciousness is a possibility for all souls. It is not only a possibility; it is the destiny and birthright of every soul. For most souls, the challenge is to be in the world but not of it, to see the three-dimensional world for what it is. In so doing there is a natural inclination to pull away from certain worldly activities that tend to emphasize attachment to systems, organizations, and things. You find time to read an inspiring book, listen to good music, write or create artwork, or simply enjoy conversation. There are dozens of new books published monthly on a wide range of personal growth and spiritual awareness subjects offering a variety of perspectives on expanding consciousness. You might join a spiritual sharing list on the internet where people from around the world offer insights about their walk on the pathway of awakening. The internet is burgeoning with such lists and sharing opportunities. Or, it might be refreshing to just take a walk in the garden, the park, or the woods to observe and feel the oneness and connectedness with life.

It is impossible to fully describe what soul consciousness

really is. Only through the actual experience of transformation from worldly consciousness to total inner awareness can you *know* yourself as a soul and *know* what soul consciousness is.

It is important to stress that *the true pathway to soul consciousness lies within the very experience you are having at any moment.* The opportunity to apply what you know, to manifest a condition consistent with your understanding of the Attributes of the Soul is always present. Every condition of your experience will respond to the purity of the love and light you infuse into the situation. It is through applying what you understand and remaining consistent in your intent that the doorway to soul consciousness remains wide open.

Though all souls are ultimately on the same path, in each soul's pattern of development it appears that there are many paths. The desire and need of the soul determines the experience; the experience defines the steps along the path; the path leads to junctures with other souls as the common path of destiny is followed leading to awakening to soul consciousness. It is necessary that we help each other arrive at the common destination. For remember, *we are all one.*

As you awaken, you know you are a soul, embodied for a time, experiencing life, learning, remembering. You walk through life radiating love and light in harmony and peace with yourself and all others. You live each moment enthusiastically, full of joy. You walk in balance and harmony along the pathway of service. Every thought, word, and action reflects the Truth you have awakened to. You know who you are. You have awakened!

9
THE PLAY OF LIFE

You no doubt find the environment you live in interesting for it is the environment created by you! This is sometimes a difficult concept to perceive, and even more difficult to accept, but the environment in which you find yourself at any given moment is the environment you have created in order to understand, learn and grow through certain lessons of life. You have created your own unique Play of Life.

In addition to being the creator, you are the observer, the coach, the actor, and the critic. You are the teacher as well as the student involved in every aspect of the play. You have created different scenes and a variety of acts. You have developed the stage arrangement, settings and props. You have attracted various people who assist in acting out the adventure and drama in the play you have created.

You also direct the play. You actively arrange the components of the play into proper relationships. You then become the audience and watch the play unfold. You observe it. You interact and become involved with what you are observing. When a particular scene has ended, you then become the critic. You feel something about the completed scene and you analyze it and then once again become the creator and producer of the next or scene.

This is an interesting way to look at how you are going through your life moment by moment for everything you create, you experience, and everything you experience, you have created. As you become aware of this pattern of life, you find there are three aspects of the *real you* within each moment of the production.

First, you are presenting *who you think you are* based upon many lifetimes of experiences and your current perception of who you are. You have written the play projecting certain intentions and requirements for the production. You have identified certain experiences and lessons to be learned for the current lifetime. You have set up scenes where you will interact with other actors and characters of the play so you can fulfill the requirements you chose. You observe and participate in life to refine your understanding, perception, and inner observation of who you think you are.

The second aspect of you in your play of life is what *the assumed you* projects into the world reacting and responding to the scenes being acted out. You project who you think you are with confidence based on your reference points in your mind and emotions. Quite often this part of your play is disassociated from the intention that initiated the play. This is the part that reflects the ego and mental activity. This is the part of you that is observing, participating, and becoming very much involved with the scene-by-scene evolution of the production you have put in motion.

It is in this process that you become emotionally attached to objects, to things, to ideas, to people, to observations. You become intellectually involved in the analysis of the result of the play. You have been so involved in reacting to the play that you have forgotten what the real purpose of the play is. When this part of you comes to a point of frustration or meets a blank wall of emotional understanding, there is often a breakthrough. There might be a feeling of lack of fulfillment. This is when you, as the observer and participant, look at what is happening and feel there has to be something more. What is behind this play of life? What is the ultimate meaning of this play? At that point, the third part of the production begins to come into focus.

The third part of you in your play of life is the *real you*, the part of you that lies dormant waiting to be recognized, waiting to be expressed. This is the you that is the true star of the production. This is the you that is the full statement of who you really are as a soul. This is the you that can walk onto the stage of life and with confidence present who you really are. This is where you apply and integrate your understanding of being fully conscious and one with the production. You are one with the moment-by-moment scenes. You are one as the observer, the audience and the critic, all saying a star is born. This is you presenting you to the world from the perspective of soul consciousness. This is you consciously walking the pathway of being love and light. You are the acclaimed star of your play, fully integrated and awakened to soul consciousness.

So you see, there are these three aspects of who you are as you produce, act, observe and respond to the environment that you create. As you internalize, identify with and understand what has been suggested as the play of life, you will find that you will look more discreetly at how you are organizing and directing your play. You will begin to observe each moment more critically. You will be aware of what you are saying, how you are reacting, how you are interacting, what you are giving attention to, and what you are consciously presenting and projecting into the environment you have created. Your environment is very dynamic, molded by and responding to the aura and energy pattern of what you project.

The play of life is not a static snapshot. It is a fluid ongoing presentation of who you think you are, who you respond as, and finally a statement of who you know you really are. So consider your environment for it is a reflection of what you are producing from within. Your created environment is your stage where you present the star of the show, the *real you*, to the world.

As you awaken to soul consciousness, you realize you are the complete statement of the perceived you, the projected you, and the real you. You are truly the star of the production presenting exactly who you really are with every thought, every word and every action. You move toward fulfillment of the cycle of learning within your created environment. You progress toward graduation as you experience any remaining lessons in the scenes of the current play you have created. This is a time of fulfillment, a time of completion, a time of graduation. The angels are applauding your progress, are you? What if you awakened to soul consciousness...*and graduated?*

10
WHAT IF.......?

What if all that you could possibly imagine about life were really true? What if you were free from limitations in life that you have created and carried with you for so long? What if you were free from doubt, fear, stress and anxiety? What if you really felt love constantly radiating from your entire being? You have always had a question about the underlying foundation of reality. What if you discovered that you, as a soul, are part of that foundation? Perhaps you should consider possibilities that lie beyond the veil of illusion that has limited your perception to three-dimensional thinking and acting. What if you lifted that veil and saw life for what it really is?

What would occur in your relationships if there were an openness to accept, to understand, to know, and to allow others to be exactly who they are? What if you had no limiting thoughts and emotions that say this can't be so, I can't do it, or it is not possible? There is unlimited potential to be experienced as we move beyond the boundaries of three-dimensional existence. It is important to remember that all limitations on awakening to soul consciousness are self imposed. Limitations are the result of holding on to memories and attachments to past events of life.

What if you lived the contemplative life and meditated daily? Everything is possible. Your existence is exactly what you create. What if you applied what you know, what you *really* know about who you are, each step along your pathway? What if you remembered that you, as a soul, are a radiant beam of love and light?

What if you look into the eyes of the next person you meet face to face and see only the pure love and light of creation? What if you open your infinite reservoir of love to everyone you encounter? What if you let go of fear of sharing love and doubt of not receiving love? What if you let go of the need to control and the fear of not being recognized or accepted? What if you allowed the consciousness of love to be your guiding light?

Awakening to soul consciousness is the only journey we are on. We know that our journey through many lifetimes has been one of remembering and letting go, remembering who we really are, letting go of false beliefs generated in the mind and emotions. As an awakened soul, questions about who you are that have been lying dormant are answered. Relationships are understood. A renewed enthusiasm is injected into life's activities as you sense a purpose, a joy, and an appreciation for all that is encountered. Other people are seen for who and what they are, each in their own way producing and acting out their own play of life. This clarity of vision brings freedom to you as a soul, freedom that transcends all human experience.

What an incredible feeling to know that there is only one teacher, one guide, one ultimate source of all wisdom, and that this resource is accessible within your inner awareness. All that we experience in the outer world of mental, emotional, and physical interaction is the result of what we first know within. With this understanding, we have the ultimate sense of freedom and allow the same freedom for all others.

The journey of the soul is a journey of discovery, or, put another way, a journey of remembering. The awakened soul remembers that it is one with the love and light of creation. Understanding this basic truth brings joy and meaning to life as you remember this reference point.

When your reference point in life is based on being love and light, you find that you are consistently motivated to walk a pathway of selfless service, to others and to the environment. There is no expectation of a benefit in return. The individual self called the ego disappears. The real you lives by example recognizing the connectedness of all creation. There are no conditional responses attached to the act of selfless service, only the sharing of love.

In the true act of service, all who are touched are blessed and bathed in the glow of universal love. It is like pouring water on one of those compressed sponges you sometimes see. When the water is absorbed by the sponge, it grows to maybe 50 times its original size, or more. Consider the influence on the expansion of consciousness as you remember who you are as a soul and serve others from that reference point. What if this were the normal interaction and exchange of energy between souls, to simply be love and light in service to each other? As you walk the pathway of service, you discover true happiness of the soul.

What if you discovered what real happiness is? Often in life, happiness is a response to physical, emotional, or mental stimulation. Ultimately as you awaken more completely to the truth of who you are, you realize that true happiness is not of the world. True happiness is the joy felt deeply within when you realize who you are, why you are in the current lifetime, and know that everyone you see is an embodied soul on their individual journey. You then walk through life enthusiastically, awakened and knowing oneness with all creation.

You walk the pathway of truly being love in every situation. You share light constantly through your eyes, through your smile, through your touch, through the entire inner flow of energy in the aura you project into your environment. You find great joy in this process as you make the inner connection with the ultimate sense of happiness fully awakened and knowing who you are.

Happiness in the outer realm is somewhat transitory, but inner happiness, or more accurately, joy, is an eternal quality of the soul. This is the true joy that the awakened soul knows and fully lives. Awakening to soul consciousness is the most priceless gift you can give yourself. It is a gift of freedom to experience, to learn, and to arrive at an enlightened understanding of who and why you are as a soul. This is a gift you can share through being an example as you live a life of revealed truth. You can share this gift with your family, friends and others you meet along the journey by consistently being the *real you*.

You know that all is one, and all is connected. As the momentum of awakening continues, more and more souls will join you in walking this pathway of enlightenment. Together, as we each do our part, we will help raise the consciousness of Earth as we accelerate into a millennium of peace and harmony riding on waves of love and light.

What if you awakened and knew you were part of a dramatic shift of consciousness on Earth?

What if you knew what your real purpose and destiny was for this lifetime?

What if.......?

EPILOGUE

The mystery of creation has been solved! You know why you are here in this lifetime. You are here to remember that you are a radiant spark of the Consciousness of Creation. You are here to be love and light, to promote peace and harmony by being an example of these soul qualities every moment of your existence. You are here to experience life enthusiastically, full of joy every moment, seeing the world for what it is, knowing that you are an eternal and immortal soul. Life has meaning. Every moment is very precious.

Your pathway through life is a journey, one that has taken you through innumerable experiences as you worked your way through releasing and letting go of the *stuff* of the mental, emotional and physical world. As you awaken and remember who you *really* are, you realize that your journey in the three-dimensional world is about completed. The journey of the soul goes on to new adventures, new environments, and new experiences in the realm of omni-dimensional existence. It's a fantastic journey, the only journey you are really on.

Our work in The Eye of the Sacred Wind Foundation is focused on helping those who are ready and dedicated to walking the pathway of awakening. We encourage everyone to open to an expanded inner understanding, to touch the core reality of who they are, and to recognize that they are a spark of the Consciousness of Creation. Our teaching program, publications and weekly Lessons from the Soul assist in awakening to this inner truth.

One of the core revelations and teachings of the foundation is centered on the eternal, immutable twelve Attributes of the Soul. Integrating and applying an understanding of these attributes into one's life pattern will greatly enhance one's conscious walk down the pathway of awakening.

We would love to hear from those of you who have been touched by the revelations in this book. Please feel free to contact us by email or letter. Our physical and spiritual doorways are always open. Know that you are part of a global extended family of souls who are, step-by-step, remembering and awakening to soul consciousness.

Enjoy the journey!

Contact information:

John Otis and Cheryl Hyland
The Eye of the Sacred Wind Foundation
PO Box 999
Whitefish, Montana 55937   USA

www.sacredwind.org   info@sacredwind.org

APPENDIX A

The Eye of the Sacred Wind Foundation

The concept for the project, the Eye of the Sacred Wind Foundation, is the result of over 45 years of study, learning, teaching and revelation of the process of awakening to soul consciousness. In December 1994, we were guided to move from Puerto Rico to New Mexico where we eventually settled in Taos. Several books would be written and we would embark on a project which was later to be named The Eye of the Sacred Wind Foundation. The name of the project was revealed to us in early May, 1995. Here is what was revealed in meditation:

It is most appropriate that this property be dedicated and christened with the energy vibration of the name that has been given, The Eye of the Sacred Wind. In time, you will appreciate the power of this name, the strength of this name, the depth of the meaning of this name. The concept of 'sacred' brings the energy pattern of this name into the very core of creation, for all creation is sacred. Every aspect of creation is sacred in the sense that it is motivated in creation by pure spirit, by the pure love of the Consciousness of Creation. When you use the meditation mantra and focus on the radiation of love, light and life, in those three words, you have defined sacred. This is a very important integrating concept that brings all that you are into focus.

When you speak of wind, the wind is the motion, the pattern of the flow of spirit, the flow of energy, the flow of sound, the flow of feeling. The wind is a feminine aspect of being that brings a feeling of sensitivity, calmness and quietness to the soul. At the same time it brings infinite power and strength to wherever the wind is felt and heard, and wherever the wind flows. You have stood on a mountaintop, or in an open place, or in the woods, and you have felt the wind blowing through, in, and around your very being.

You have felt and heard the wind as it caresses all of nature. It is the enveloping, caressing nurturing aspect of love, light and life. It brings forth not only the wind of the physical world but also a wind of spirit in the inner realm which when touched is felt as a caressing inner sensation, an inner knowing, an inner blessing of spirit moving in and through and nurturing every aspect of inner reality and inner creation. Consider these concepts. Meditate on what is suggested and implied by the very meaningful name of 'sacred wind' and you will know why this name has been given for the integration of activity of the work to be accomplished.

Thus the name was established, The Eye of the Sacred Wind Foundation. The Foundation offers a teaching program to provide specific and helpful guidance and information to those who are prepared and ready to look within to discover *who* and *why* they are as a soul.

The program offered provides specific insights into the makeup of the soul and the well-defined Attributes of the Soul. The Attributes are directly related to the expression of one's character and nature in this life, and are specifically related to the path one has chosen for learning and experiencing his or her real self in this lifetime. Participating in programs offered through the Foundation will offer an inner impact that can be a life-changing experience.

The programs of the Foundation provide a forum for those who desire an introduction to the pathway of awakening to soul consciousness. Several books are being published on various aspects of the awakening process and the makeup of the soul. Weekly emailed Lessons from the Soul are shared with thousands of people around the world who desire to receive these inspirational revelations from the Higher Self. In addition, we offer Destiny Awareness readings to assist those who are ready to identify and then live their chosen pathway in this lifetime.

The goal of the Foundation is to encourage you to present who you know you are to the world on a consistent basis. This is a very practical approach to a teaching of Truth. It is practical because not only when one touches the depths of understanding does it make sense, but also the application can be seen in the results, interactions, positive activity and influence the teaching has in one's life. By example one then makes a statement in life that is seen and observed by others who are then stimulated to awaken to an expanded inner truth. All is one, all is connected.

We invite you to visit our web site and to contact us directly if you feel so inclined. If you are ever in our neighborhood of Northwest Montana, please let us know. It is always a pleasure to make contact with fellow travelers on the pathway of awakening to soul consciousness.

Blessings of Love and Light,

John and Cheryl, Whitefish, Montana

APPENDIX B

About the Author

John W. Otis has had a lifelong interest and involvement in the study, discovery, and application of universal principles. He has been actively involved as a lecturer and teacher in various spiritual growth and metaphysical organizations for over 40 years. He served as Assistant Director and Teacher at the Christ Truth Foundation in Portland, Oregon during the 1970's, and since that time has been President and co-founder with his wife, Cheryl, of The Eye of the Sacred Wind Foundation.

John has been receiving guided messages from the Higher Self since 1965. These messages, or *Lessons from the Soul*, have been recorded since 1995 and are part of an extensive library maintained at the Foundation. The lessons are on a variety of subjects related to various aspects of spiritual growth and expanding awareness. John was exposed to metaphysical concepts early in life as his family was closely aligned with Edgar Cayce from 1911 until Cayce's death in 1945. John's mother had one of the earliest medical readings from Cayce when she was three years old. She was healed from polio and lived to be 95.

After graduating from Stanford University in 1960 with a BS degree in General Engineering, John served as a US Naval Officer, entrepreneur, international business educator, and world traveler. Since 1986, he has been active in educational, economic and community development projects in the United States, Central Europe and Russia. He has been the keynote speaker at international conferences and has lectured extensively on community and business development, and on spiritual growth topics. He has also published various magazine articles and books including *Will the Real You Please Stand Up?*, published in June,

2006. He also published *Whispers From the Soul* in March, 2009, a collection of inspirational reflections. John and his wife, Cheryl, currently reside in Whitefish, Montana, where they are active full time in the work of the Foundation. John is an ordained minister, soul counselor and Teacher of Truth. He officiates at weddings and other ceremonies, and offers soul counseling through destiny awareness readings.

APPENDIX C

The Higher Self

Intuition is of the soul and has no emotional or linguistic barriers that impede an understanding of eternal soul realities. When we respond to intuition, we are connecting with infinite awareness filtered into conscious reality and understanding of the moment. We tap into a universal storehouse of experience and wisdom that is one with all souls. We connect with the Higher Self.

The Higher Self is a composite of soul energy that holds all knowledge and wisdom. The Higher Self is always ready to share that which is necessary to understand or work through an experience in life. When we say *my* Higher Self we really mean *the* Higher Self. Remember, all is one, all is connected. The universal wisdom resident in the depths of soul consciousness is available to be applied as needed in every situation.

All that one experiences as part of the awakening process or learning cycle emanates from an aspect of the Higher Self that is guiding and nurturing the unfolding process. The Higher Self provides stability and insights along the way. Everything that occurs within your experience as you search for and align with the truth of your being is guided by the Higher Self.

It should always be remembered that the Higher Self is totally, irreversibly and consciously one with the Consciousness of Creation. The Higher Self is that aspect of the soul that is like the final link. It is the fuse. It is that which connects the soul with all that is part of creation. The Higher Self provides that which will be received and that which is applicable for the moment for the development of awareness to take place within the soul. Information is often provided in a conscious and very direct manner. Sometimes inner guidance is very subtle, indirect and subconscious, such as when you receive those little nudges, aha's, and flashes of intuition that occur when you are sensing on some level the movement of energy, the movement of spirit, the movement of the love, light and life of creation through your immediate experience. The Higher Self is the highest point of consciousness within the soul, the final link to total oneness with the Consciousness of Creation. The Higher Self is the source of intuition, a guardian on the pathway of consciousness. Ultimately the Higher Self is the pinnacle of focus through which the consciousness of the soul is fully realized. All experiences leads toward unification with the Higher Self, the true consciousness of who you are as a soul.

APPENDIX D

What is a Soul?

It is important to remember that all creation is cyclical. It is a pattern of energy moving out, circulating, and returning. As you keep this principle of creative energy in focus, it becomes easier to understand the process and to know the purpose for which the three-dimensional world exists. It is through three-dimensional existence that you experience the process as well as the result of creation.

There is a pattern that can perhaps be expressed in words that will resonate with your inner awareness. It is a pattern through which the creative process moves. First there is an impulse. The impulse moves through the mind, becomes an idea, a thought, and then the creative process moves into manifested form and substance. All creation, all patterns of creative energy begin with a thought, with an idea, with an impulse from the depths of inner awareness. As the creative energy moves out, there is form and substance. Look around you at all that has been created in the physical world, in the world of emotions, in the world of the intellect and the mind. There is an infinite array of created form and substance. It has always been this way; it will always be this way.

When you consider the process of creation, have you ever wondered who or what is a soul? Why does a soul exist? What is the soul really all about? This is a question that is at the very core of all spiritual pursuit and must be answered. As you look around you at your beautiful surroundings, the earth, the plants, the animals, and of course humankind, there are many thoughts and ideas you might have as to how this universe, or any other universe, came to be.

The first thought, the first flow of energy into the creative experience is love. In the process of creation, the concept of love becomes a living reality. Love is a word that is not easily understood, for it means many things to many people who, in their own way, are awakening to the truth of their existence. Love is all encompassing, has many faces, and is the totality of the expression of creative energy. It is for this reason that it has been said that love is the Source. It has been said that God, or the Consciousness of Creation is love...which is true!

As the impulse of love moves out into the void of the universe, there is a presentation of the creative essence that is sustained through the radiant expressive energy patterns seen in the created universe.

Love is carried into creation on the energy wave of light. Light is the foundation or the active ingredient of the impulse of creation. Light is the animating force that, through the creative process, forms what is called life. Love is the source, light is the activating principle, life is the result.

As the energy of love moves on waves of light, there are packets of energy that come together as points of consciousness to participate within the creative process. These sparks of energy are called souls. These entities, or souls, are created aspects of the Consciousness of Creation, and carry forth the experience of creation, sharing and radiating the love and light of the Source.

When a child is conceived it is a combination of the physical attributes and qualities of each of its parents. In the same way, the soul that enters that child is an aspect of and a part of the very essence of the Consciousness of Creation. The soul is the divine essence of creation that carries with it all of the attributes or qualities of the infinite expression of the Consciousness of Creation.

The soul is the creative impulse of the universe in motion,

creating and exploring that which is created. These creative impulses, or souls, have moved into and through various dimensions of existence to eventually be embodied in three-dimensional existence. In this process the worlds were created, the physical universe and eventually the individualized units of energy called planets were created. Then life forms were created and the ongoing creative essence of the universe became the physical reality in which you now find yourself.

The truth of creation, the truth of existence, the truth of the Consciousness of Creation as a radiant energy pattern of love and light can then be known. In understanding this truth, the doorway is opened to the singular truth of the universe and all creation. Everything is connected, nothing stands alone. You, as a soul, are a spark of the Consciousness of Creation, connected to all that exists.

Along the way, the soul became involved with, attached to, and enamored by that which was created. This attachment became the anchor of assumed reality considered by the soul to be the purpose for having been created in the first place. However, when the pinnacle of understanding is reached, it is seen and known that the created environment is symbolic. It is the result of that which is the creative impulse. The created environment is not the absolute reality of existence.

Through attachment, lessons are learned; lessons of acceptance, of release, of letting go. One begins to understand the lessons which are created by the mind and emotions, the lessons that open the doorway to inner soul awareness. This leads to letting go and returning to that which is the inner truth and reality of soul existence. This is the process and the purpose for all aspects of creation. There is movement of creative energy, form and substance come into being, and there is attachment to the form and substance. Lessons are learned, there is then a releasing and letting go. There is a return to that which is the Source, the oneness of all existence.

It is not an overly complicated process, but is made so by the infinite array of perceptions that souls maintain regarding what is observed in the omni-dimensional, infinite, created universe, and more specifically within the localized three-dimensional experience. Observe all around you. Observe and feel what is being processed in understanding from deep within your consciousness as a soul. Know that as you release and let go, as you become unattached, as you turn your focus inward rather than outward, the pathway home, the pathway of return to the full and unified consciousness of oneness is assured. This will always be the return pathway of every soul. To live in the midst of the created environment and to consciously know the truth of who you are is the ultimate lesson that every soul must pass through.

You are living in conscious reality. You are a soul temporarily utilizing bodily form to learn, to experience, to remember. You are learning to become unattached to that which you experience as you move into the inner realm, into the full and complete unified consciousness of oneness of who you are as a soul.

So congratulations! You are a master creator! As you move along the pathway of creation, acknowledge and understand that which you have created. Bless each step, give thanks for each step. Acknowledge and recognize that you are offering yourself a gift with each step, a gift of another key to the doorway of awakening. Observe what you have created and know that you have done so for only one purpose: to experience what is created, then move beyond the limitations of the created environment to consciously unite with the one Source, the Consciousness of Creation. Integrate this understanding with each step you take through the environment you have created!

APPENDIX E

Attributes of the Soul

Following are the Attributes of the Soul and their
numerical equivalent.

1 - Spirit

2 - Beauty

3 - Might

4 - Harmony

5 - Life

6 - Truth

7 - Intelligence

8 - Image

9 - Reality

10 - Opulence

11 - Light

12 - Principle

13 - Soul Consciousness

For a more in depth discussion of the Attributes, please see
Chapter 4: The Soul, Part Two.

APPENDIX F

Finding Your Destiny Path

Every soul has a purpose for being. There is always a reason for every event one experiences in life. Often the reason is not evident or clear, but there are no mistakes. Every event, every choice is part of the ever-unfolding expansion of consciousness of the soul. This includes the choice to enter into a certain lifetime to gain additional experience.

To recognize one's true spiritual destiny during one's lifetime and then to consciously apply what is known to every aspect of experience, is indeed a pinnacle of achievement for the soul. By understanding one's chosen destiny path, a soul can consciously and productively make great progress on its spiritual journey. The soul begins to focus on those areas that are reflective of the primary purpose for the current experience. These are generally the areas in need of refinement or balancing in order to obtain the absolute purity of motivation, purity of intent, and purity of application in all aspects of life.

As one goes through life, particularly with the advantage of several years of experience, it becomes apparent that there is a pattern unfolding. There is a connectedness, though perhaps vague at times, between the events of one's life and the lessons that one seems to be learning. This is one of life's *aha's* when one realizes that there does seem to be a destiny pattern unfolding. There seems to be a direction, or perhaps a goal toward which one is heading. There seems to be something that one is *destined* to do or to be!

The birth path of a soul reflects the destiny pattern for the selected lifetime. When a soul comes into the world, there is indeed a certain energy pattern in place as well as a timing sequence initiated that is quite unique for a given soul. Everything is connected. As the soul begins its current journey, everything necessary for the fulfillment of the chosen path of soul development is in place. The family, future friends, forthcoming events, and various learning situations that will require discernment and decision-making are all in place. The pattern best suited for soul awareness in the current lifetime has been chosen and put into motion. It is indeed a useful step for a soul to become aware of this pattern, to become aware of the potential inherent in every condition of life for learning and for advancement in soul consciousness. Through this awareness, it is then possible to consciously apply what one knows to every activity. One can begin to see within the outcome of every relationship and event the lessons needed to bring one back to the middle road of applying and living the fullness of the Attributes of the Soul.

It should not be too surprising that the chosen date of birth deeply reflects the energy pattern of the soul as it comes into the three-dimensional world. For anyone who has had even a passing exposure to astrology, the relationship between the date of birth and the chosen pattern for life can be seen and understood.

There is a rhythm to both the observed, or seen, and the unseen aspects of the universe. When a soul enters the world as a newborn child, there is an imprint of an energy pattern that resonates within the soul. This energy pattern provides the foundation for embarking upon the current life journey. The soul is positioned to maximize its pursuit of experiencing that which is necessary to bring about the learning cycle desired. Whether this happens or not in a given lifetime, or whether one is conscious of the process or not, is up to the individual soul. We are in an age of transition when more and more souls entering into the earth experience are coming prepared to do that which is necessary to become fully conscious. This is a time for completing the circle, or from the teachings of the indigenous peoples, a time to mend the medicine wheel.

When consciously aware of one's chosen destiny path, decisions are made, understandings developed, and actions are taken within the context of a greater perspective. There is never a question of the eventual destiny of the soul; we are all, as souls, on the pathway of return to conscious union with the One, the Consciousness of Creation. *From the One comes many; from the many comes One.* The only question is whether the soul will make choices in the current life that are consistent with progressing down the chosen destiny path.

The birth (destiny) path can be decoded to reveal the particular Attribute of the Soul that has been chosen to work within the present experience. The goal is to experience and then understand the qualities of the particular attribute as revealed through application of decisions and choices in the current lifetime. The destiny path reveals *what* a soul has chosen to work on, to perfect in understanding, and to refine in application. Through understanding the chosen birth path attribute, the soul will come to a greater understanding of how that particular attribute connects with the other attributes. In fulfilling the current destiny path, not only will past karma be erased, but it will become increasingly clear how the twelve Attributes of the Soul combine in the fullness of soul consciousness.

The name path, on the other hand, describes the *how* of one's life, or more particularly, the method by which one has chosen to fulfill the intended destiny pattern. The name path is unique for every soul, particularly when interpreted in conjunction with the destiny path. It applies to past experience as well as current chosen directions for learning the lessons of life. The name one chooses is uniquely accurate as it reveals the inner motivation and inner impulses that drive one's decisions, thoughts, and activities. Through reflecting on the name from the point of view of the Attributes of the Soul, one discovers the hidden truth of one's being. One begins to understand why certain conditions are experienced. One then responds from a soul perspective which greatly accelerates the progress of spiritual awakening.

When approached from the perspective of soul awareness, a clear relationship can be discovered between the name chosen at birth, and the Attributes of the Soul chosen to be more clearly understood in the current lifetime. Usually there is one attribute that best defines the life path. Other attributes are implied or are seen to be related through the frequency with which they are revealed in the components of the chosen birth name. As one progresses through life and assumes new names, nicknames, or other modifications to the birth name, new and expanded aspects of the journey of the soul are revealed through the attributes associated with the modified name. In every case, the name or names chosen by a soul will reveal the areas of focus selected by the soul for optimizing spiritual growth.

It must be remembered that all paths of experience lead toward awakening to the fullness of soul consciousness. Whether consciously recognized and acknowledged or not, the soul is always proceeding toward a reuniting with the Source. A soul has constant exposure to the experiences and vicissitudes of life that provide the foundation for expanding in awareness. As the soul applies the necessary energy, one works on the selected Attributes of the Soul and understanding is refined.

The destiny path reveals the areas of chosen focus for a conscious progression in spiritual awareness to take place. The classroom of the earthly school provides the environment for learning the lessons needed. *There is no other way to advance in consciousness.* A soul needs to be part of the earth experience to learn progressively that which is needed to become the fully conscious embodiment of the Attributes of the Soul.

The inner pathway *can* be discovered. Understanding how one has been positioned to learn particular lessons can be most helpful. The conditions for the entrance of the soul into the earth experience are basically selected by the entering soul. These conditions include all the parameters of the point of entrance including parents, given name, time and place of birth, and conditions that will influence the chosen lifetime. The name at birth is most important for it describes the energy pattern of the soul in terms of how it will subconsciously, and often consciously, approach life's choices and decisions. The name reveals the particular soul attribute (or attributes) chosen as the central focus.

It should be remembered that the journey of the soul is always happening. There is never a time when the soul is not facing itself, looking into the mirror of both current and past experience. As one moves through the excitement of life involved in all that attracts and often holds one in the physical, emotional, or mental realm, there are repeated opportunities for direct application of one's understanding of the soul attributes chosen for focus in the current lifetime.

Once again, there is always the freedom of choice, the freedom to follow the impulses from within the soul, as well as the freedom to follow the worldly patterns of outer experience. The birth path and the name path only point the way for the current lifetime. They define the opportunity and chosen applications that would be best followed to truly understand and integrate the Attributes of the Soul into one's consciousness. The choice is up to the individual soul. Choices are made daily, even momentarily, as one comes face to face with their own created reality and lessons to be learned. Whether or not one learns the chosen lessons is up to the individual soul. The doorway is opened, but the soul needs to consciously walk through.

The inner journey is most significant; it is unavoidable. The only difference between one who lives, responds, and exists in external conditions and one who lives, responds, and exists within the reality of inner understandings, is one of consciousness.

ॐ

For more information on Destiny Awareness Readings, please see our web site: www.sacredwind.org.

LANGUAGE OF THE SOUL

Glossary of Terms

Androgynous   The result of merging masculine and
                       feminine energy into a unified whole,
                       two as one.

**Attributes of   The twelve immutable, eternal qualities
the Soul**   or attributes of creation residing within the
                       soul, the composite statement of soul reality.

Awakening   The process of becoming aware of the omni-
                       dimensional nature of the soul, the process
                       of recognizing the soul as the Consciousness
                       of Creation in motion.

Awareness   The *knowing* quality of consciousness, omni-
                       dimensional perception, knowing that you
                       know.

Connectedness   The conscious linking of all elements of
                       creation in recognition of there being one
                       Source of all.

Consciousness   The energy of creation, the energy of
                       knowing, the energy of being.

**Consciousness of   The source consciousness of all creation
Creation**   on all dimensions of existence, the All in
                       All, the One, God, Allah, the Great Mystery,
                       the underlying reality of an always present
                       infinite creative energy.

Higher Self	The universal storehouse of experience and wisdom that is one with all souls, a composite of soul energy that holds all knowledge and wisdom, the doorway or link with the Consciousness of Creation.
Incarnation	The movement of soul energy into manifested form for the purpose of experiencing and understanding omni-dimensional creation.
Intuition	Inner knowing, an impulse from the soul as guidance, the inner voice.
Love	The Source of all creation, the Consciousness of Creation.
Light	The carrier wave of love energy into creation, the energy of consciousness in motion.
Light Body	The composite statement of light energy in every cell of consciousness of the soul, the bridge between the physical (life) and the root energy of all creation (love).
Life	The result of love and light moving into manifestation along the infinite continuum of creation.
Oneness	The consciousness of unity and connectedness of all creation, knowing the common source and energy of all creation.

Quantum Physics	Quantum physics is the branch of physics based on quantum theory which is the theoretical basis of modern physics that explains the nature and behavior of matter and energy on the atomic and subatomic level.
Soul	The creative impulse of the universe in motion, the energy of love, light, and life being manifested, a spark of the divine essence of creation, the eternal and immortal aspect of self that has within its makeup all the qualities or attributes of the Consciousness of Creation.
Soul Consciousness	Awareness of *who* you are as a soul, consciously aligned with the Attributes of the Soul, and living the truth of who you are as revealed from within.
Soul Memory	The imprint within the consciousness of the soul of experiences in prior lifetimes that define the intention and purpose for the current lifetime including lessons to be learned in order to fully awaken to soul consciousness.
Soul Library	Information within the consciousness of the soul related to past soul experiences and the reservoir of universal truth available for reference as the soul expands in awareness of its true character and nature.

Soulmates	The conscious merging of two souls as one in recognition from within of the unity of all consciousness.
Trinity	The foundational principle of creation: mother/father/child, masculine/feminine/androgynous, Love/Light/Life.
Unity	The conscious blending of creative energy as a harmonious whole.

Breinigsville, PA USA
19 May 2010
238338BV00003B/78/P